FRONTIER JUSTICE
IN THE WILD WEST

FRONTIER JUSTICE
IN THE WILD WEST

BUNGLED, BIZARRE, AND FASCINATING EXECUTIONS

R. MICHAEL WILSON

TWODOT®

GUILFORD, CONNECTICUT
HELENA, MONTANA
AN IMPRINT OF THE GLOBE PEQUOT PRESS

A · T W O D O T® · B O O K

Copyright © 2007 by R. Michael Wilson

Text design by Lisa Reneson, Two Sisters Design
Map by Lisa Reneson © Morris Book Publishing, LLC

Library of Congress Cataloging-in-Publication Data is available on file.
ISBN 978-0-7627-4389-6
Printed in the United States of America
10 9 8 7 6 5 4

To the victims, so oft forgotten

Vancouver
Island

British Columbia

Alberta

Saskatchewan

Manitoba

WASHINGTON

OREGON

MONTANA

NORTH DAKOTA

• Idaho
  City

IDAHO

Sheridan •

• Deadwood

SOUTH DAKOTA

WYOMING

Yankton •

Elko •

Ogden •

NEBRASKA

Virginia City •

• Salt Lake

Cheyenne

Carson •

Murray •   City

Sandy •

NEVADA

UTAH

• Denver

COLORADO

CALIFORNIA

• Mountain
  Meadows

KANSAS

• Peach Springs
• Prescott

Clayton •

OKLAHOMA

ARIZONA

NEW MEXICO

Tombstone •

Bisbee •

TEXAS

MEXICO

N

Contents

Acknowledgments

It is always a pleasure after a book has been researched, compiled, written and copyedited, to acknowledge those organizations that have made the work possible. *Frontier Justice* is no exception and could not have been completed without the support and assistance of the following:

The American Medical Association Archives; the Arizona State Historical Society; the Arizona Territorial Prison Historic State Park; the Carbon County (Wyoming) Museum; the Colorado State Historical Society; the Denver (Colorado) Public Library; the Idaho State Historical Society; the Nebraska State Historical Society; the Nevada State Archives; the Nevada State Historical Society; the Rio Grande County (Colorado) Museum; Sharlot Hall Museum in Prescott, Arizona; the South Dakota State Historical Society; the Utah History Research Center; and the Wyoming State Archives. Special recognition is due to artist Eileen Hayes Skibo.

Introduction

FRONTIER JUSTICE WAS COMPARATIVELY SWIFT, usually fair, and frequently brutal. On the frontier, justice took many forms, and hanging was arguably the most popular. The practice of hanging heinous criminals came to America with the Europeans and continued into the western territories with the pioneers. Typically, only premeditated first-degree murder resulted in a legal execution; to accommodate lesser crimes, lighter punishments were devised. Contrary to popular belief, vigilantes usually applied justice with the same overarching set of constraints.

As the population of the West swelled and towns sprang up overnight, jails were often the last structures erected. Petty criminals could be held under close guard for short periods in any secure structure, but in those early days it was more practical to chain a man to a rock, heavy log, or tree. Minor offenses could also be effectively curtailed by banishing the wrongdoer. As an example, soon after Cheyenne, Wyoming, was established in 1868, one of the local newspapers published a list of undesirable characters along with a warning that they either leave town or face the wrath of the vigilantes. The "posted" men packed their belongings and moved westward to the Union Pacific Railroad's end of the track at Laramie.

Offenses such as selling liquor to Indians generally resulted in brutal, though not lethal, treatment. On January 4, 1880, the *Virginia City (Nevada) Territorial Enterprise* reported that Tom Rogers had been selling whiskey to Indians near Reno, Nevada. He had been flogged for this offense and ordered to leave town. Rogers did not heed the warning, however, and the citizens promptly captured him, rode him around town on a rail, and then applied tar and feathers.

The same punishment had been meted out to W. J. Jones in Reno fifteen months earlier. Jones, who had a profitable wholesale liquor business called Hedge & Company, had established an illegal still and earned a reputation as one of the most skillful "mixers" in the trade. The citizens of Reno, determined to put an end to Jones's illegal activities, tarred and feathered him before sending him out on the westbound train for Truckee, California. On September 22, 1878, the *Truckee Republican* reported:

> We saw the victim Thursday night on the overland train. He was in a truly pitiable condition. Coal tar, or gas tar, had been used, and used freely. This substance blisters like a mustard plaster. The cuticle will peel off of Mr. Jones just as if he had been boiled. His hair and the wound on his head was filled with tar. The hair stuck out in all directions, or at least a mass of tar stuck out. The sockets of his eyes were level full with solid tar, which seemed to have been poured into them and allowed to cool. His whiskers seemed a large, unshapely mass of tar. His face, neck, and, we are told, his entire body, had a thick coating. The Vigilantes kindly clothed him before putting him on the train. The sight might have been ludicrous, if it had not been agonizing. The train was nearly three hours in reaching Truckee. The

pain endured by the poor fellow was excruciating. Sightless, helpless, coated with a horrid, odoriferous substance, he sat silently, with his head bowed over. Occasionally his fingers would grasp spasmodically at the open air. Sometimes his body would twitch nervously, as if from the pain he endured. Arriving at Truckee, Grandison Jones [no relation] and another colored man were put to work to remove the tar. It was an hour before Dr. R. J. Goss was called and the linseed oil which he prescribed obtained. Everybody who saw the poor wretch pitied him. The very men who performed the deed would have pitied him. His sufferings were extreme. His eyes were fairly burning up. No one ever heard before of putting tar on a man's face and in his eyes. For six hours two men worked faithfully neutralizing the tar and removing it from his body. We saw him this morning. His eyes were terribly inflamed. It is doubtful if he ever recovers his sight. It is feared the eye balls have been burned and blistered and forever destroyed.

Clearly, it was not unusual for vigilantes to veer toward the gruesome and sadistic in devising punishments for lawbreakers. When a man was suspected of a crime, it was all too common a practice to bind his wrists and ankles, place a noose about his neck, and hoist him up until he was unconscious. He would then be lowered, revived, and questioned until he confessed. Some prisoners braved this ordeal three or four times, and only weakened when told that the next "lift" would be their last if they did not say what was desired. John Burns spoke from personal experience:

Some time during the war ruffians, who desired to be thought [bush] whackers, came upon me at my house, intending to compel me to give up some money I was supposed to have. I had none, and told them so, but they did not believe me and their next move was to cut a cord out of a bedstead, tie one end around my neck, throw the other over a joist overhead, and pull me up till my feet were clear of the floor. This they did four times, questioning me between whiles. I lost consciousness every time as soon as my feet left the floor but felt no pain at any time, and after the second hoist I meant to sham continued insensibility when they let me drop again, since to lower me they just let go the rope and I fell to the floor, but this was beyond my power. My first consciousness was that I had raised my body to a sitting position, which put shamming out of the question. I experienced no pain when the rope tightened, nor when I was suspended, nor after I was released, except the soreness caused on my skin by the chafing of the rope.

In contrast to a legal execution, a person hanged in a lynching experienced a slow process of strangulation similar to that which occurred in a suicide by hanging. In 1872 a Paris *Gaulois* correspondent, determined to end it all, drove a nail into a wall, attached a loop of cord, stood on a chair, and placed his head in the noose. After kicking the chair away, he hung from his self-made noose until he was saved by a friend, who arrived unexpectedly and held him until the rope could be cut down. The correspondent was revived and later related his experience in an article titled "How It Feels To Be Hanged":

The immediate consequent sensation was very strange. From the soles of my feet to the crown of my head a sort of general mixing up of the fluids of the body ensued. Suddenly there flashed before my eyes a sparkling, dancing light of a color which was difficult to describe, but in which a sober red predominated. Presently the flashing light concentrated at a single focus, and thence spread away into space in ripples such as are made in a pond when a stone is cast into it. At the same time a fearful weight pressed upon my head—a compression, as if my temples were tightly bound in a ring of iron. My hands and feet were full of pins and needles. Needles without number seemed to pass out of the ends of my fingers by a process of continual expulsion. Then came a terrible "snapping" at the nape of my neck, and along my spine there passed a wriggling which I could only compare to a small serpent forcing a passage along the vertebrae. My last sensation was one of acute pain at the throat and shoulder blades, and finally came a state of perfect unconsciousness.

In the earliest days of western frontier justice, legal hangings were conducted using a stout limb and a rope. A wagon and team were used to launch the condemned person into eternity. This method was no more effective than a lynching, as it provided no drop to dislocate the vertebrae. As a result, several early hangings were badly bungled affairs. In New Mexico, for instance, the first legal hanging of a woman on the frontier was a fiasco from beginning to end.

Pablita Sandoval had murdered her lover, a married man with five children. Sentenced to hang, and ordered to pay the cost of her execution and burial, she was led out of her cell on April 26, 1861, by Sheriff Antonio Herrera. He seated the woman on her coffin in a wagon, then drove the wagon beneath a limb, hurriedly adjusted the noose, jumped back onto the wagon seat, and whipped up the horses. Only at that moment did the sheriff realize that he had neglected to bind Sandoval's arms and legs. As she struggled to pull herself up, the sheriff, using all his weight, pulled down on her legs. Several outraged spectators cut the rope before the sheriff warned them off with his six-shooter. The death warrant, which required that Sandoval be "hanged until dead," was read, and the sheriff backed the team under the limb again and tied another noose. He lifted Sandoval into the wagon, pinioned her arms and legs, and held her up until the noose was adjusted. He took but a moment to examine his work before driving the wagon out a second time. This time around, the law was satisfied.

In later legal executions, the goal was a quick, humane death. This was accomplished in a hanging by the violent dislocation of the cervical vertebrae. One of the most distasteful duties during an execution was to spring the trapdoor or release the counterpoise weight, and thus initiate the hanging process. Various means were devised over time to relieve a person of that duty. When Tom Horn was hanged in 1903, Cheyenne architect James P. Julian designed a device whereby the weight of the condemned man upon the trapdoor sprang a plug from a washbasin. When the water flowed out, the weight of sandbags on the opposite side tipped a lever that pulled the support for the trapdoor.

The rope used in hangings was typically made of hemp because the strands were longer and stronger than flax. The rope had to be thick enough so that, even after stretching, it wouldn't cut into the condemned's neck. To remove elasticity, the rope was soaked in water and stretched by a heavy weight. It was always tested for the condemned's weight, usually by dropping a comparable weight the required distance through the trapdoor. The loops of the noose were not a set number, but seven loops were most often used—though on occasion a hangman might use anywhere from five to thirteen. The noose was lubricated—usually with soap, grease, or wax—to facilitate sliding and cinching of the rope.

After the noose was positioned around the neck of the condemned, the knot was placed under the left ear. This caused the head to snap backward, dislocating the vertebrae. If the knot was placed under the right ear, the head would snap forward and a slow strangulation would occur. Typically, a hanged man remained suspended until an attending physician pronounced him dead.

Every hanging was unique, but Dr. D. S. Lamb, an ex-surgeon of the United States Army who studied the subject, reported on the three "stages through which the victim passes" in an 1894 issue of the *St. Louis Globe-Democrat:*

> In the first stage the victim passes into a partial stupor last-
> ing from thirty seconds to two minutes, but this is generally gov-
> erned by the length of the drop, the weight of the body, and the
> tightness of the constriction. There is absolutely no pain in this
> stage; the feeling is rather one of pleasure. The subjective symp-
> toms described are intense heat in the head, brilliant flashes of
> light in the eyes, deafening sounds in the ears and a heavy numb
> feeling in the lungs. In the second stage the subject passes into
> unconsciousness and convulsions usually occur. In the third
> stage all is quiet except the beating of the heart. Just before death
> the agitation is renewed, but in a different way from that in the
> second state. The feet are raised, the tongue has a peculiar spasm,
> the chest heaves, the eyes protrude from the orbits and oscillate
> from side to side, and the pupils dilate. The pulse can, in most
> cases, be felt ten minutes after the drop.

This three-stage process depended upon the rope being properly knotted and adjusted. When carefully positioned on the left
shoulder just behind the jaw, the knot presses upon the carotid artery,
cutting off blood to the brain. This results in unconsciousness in a
matter of seconds. Ideally, during a legal hanging, the spine would be
dislocated between the first and second or the second and third cervical vertebrae. The spinal cord would be severed—or at least severely
compressed—and all sensation to the torso and extremities would be
cut off.

In the following pages you will read about some of the most
thrilling and unusual cases of frontier justice recorded in the annals of
the Old West, from the assassination of "Wild Bill" Hickok at a
Deadwood poker table to the sordid story of "Big Nose" George Parrott,

who was hanged and then skinned—and whose "hide" was fashioned into a pair of shoes worn by Wyoming governor John Osborne.

In all there were more than one thousand men and two women legally executed on the western frontier before 1910. There were also countless deaths from extralegal proceedings, some following elaborate people's court hearings and others from spontaneous responses to outrageous public offenses. From among the many incidents of frontier justice, some events stand out as unique or peculiar, and what follows are some of the more noteworthy examples of justice administered on America's western frontier.

Frenchman Hanged for Murdering a "Lady"

April 24, 1868

JULIA "JULE" BULETTE WAS DESCRIBED by the *Virginia City (Nevada) Territorial Enterprise* as "frail but fair." She had come to New Orleans from London, England, and had left behind a brother and uncle in Louisiana when she traveled west. By 1853 she had made her way to California; ten years later she arrived in Virginia City. Thirty-five-year-old Bulette, a "woman of the town," was characterized by the *Enterprise* as being of a "very kind-hearted, liberal, benevolent and charitable disposition." A "prostitute with a heart of gold," Bulette had been elected an honorary member of Virginia City's Fire Engine Company No. 1, in recognition of "munificent gifts bestowed by her upon the company." She took a great interest in all matters connected with the fire department, and even worked the brakes on the engines sent to respond to several fires.

On the evening of Saturday, January 19, 1867, Jule entertained a man believed to be a miner. They were in her small house near the corner of D and Union Streets, just a stone's throw from the fire station house. The miner was long gone when Bulette's houseboy entered her home at eleven o'clock the next morning to make the fire, stock the

1

woodpile, sweep, and generally clean up. Bulette lay in bed, the covers pulled over her, and the houseboy was as quiet as possible to allow her to sleep late. She didn't stir during the entire time he was there. At noon Gertrude Holmes, who lived next door, called Bulette for breakfast. When she received no response, she entered by the back door and found Jule in bed, bloody and lifeless. Holmes wasted no time raising the alarm.

J. S. Kaneen was the first man to respond to the scene. He found Jule "lying with her head in the middle of the bed, while her feet were outside of the bed, and nearly against the wall of the room. Her clothes were lying on the floor beside the bed as though she had simply dropped them in undressing and stepped out of them into bed. The bed on both sides of the deceased looked perfectly smooth, no one evidently having occupied it with her." According to the *Enterprise:*

> Kaneen found a short stick of cedar firewood lying on a box of fuel in the room, which had some wool from the blanket upon it and there were also some splinters of cedar bark upon the bed clothes. On the side of her head was a bruise, and splinters and chips of wood were in her hair and on her temple . . . Jule was lying on her left side with a pillow over her head and face, the bed clothes beneath her head being saturated with blood. Her throat was lacerated with the marks of finger nails, and the blood suffused and distorted countenance, together with the writhing position of the body, showed conclusive evidence of strangulation. The pillow was pressed also on her head and face, evidently to silence any outcries on her part. There were two small wounds on her forehead, apparently made by the cock of a pistol or something of that character, and the back of her left hand was somewhat lacerated in her struggles to free herself.

JULIA BULETTE

At the inquest, one of the carriers for the *Enterprise* testified that at five o'clock in the morning, as he was crossing a vacant lot between D and E Streets, he heard a woman scream. He said he stopped to listen and look about, but neither hearing nor seeing anything unusual, he continued on to the Oriental Hotel. Two doctors who performed the autopsy on Bulette testified that upon removing the scalp, they found the skull uninjured. They also noted that the wounds on her forehead, from a pistol cock, were merely superficial and the official cause of death was from suffocation. An examination of the house revealed that property was missing, raising the suspicion that robbery was at least one motive.

The night after the murder as Jule lay in her casket, John Milleain, a Frenchman and generally a man of bad reputation, sat with her corpse. The officials at the fire department insisted that they should bury their honorary member, and the funeral took place at 3:00 in the afternoon, two days after her murder. The procession began from Engine House No. 1 on B Street and was well attended by sixty people. The Metropolitan Brass Band led the procession, and several mourners followed a caravan of sixteen carriages—including Milleain, who joined the firemen marching behind the carriage. Together, they marched to the gravesite at Flowery Hill Cemetery.

On May 2, 1867, an attempt was made to rob and murder Bulette's friend, Martha Camp. A man armed with a large knife had hidden in Camp's room on South C Street, and was discovered skulking about her bed, intent on murdering and robbing her. When he crept toward the bed Camp's screams sent the man running out the back door, but not before she had time to glimpse a fair view of the man's face. Soon afterward she recognized the man on C Street, and he was arrested immediately. Lodged in the county jail on a charge of attempting to rob and murder Camp, the man was soon identified as John Milleain. The same man who appeared grief stricken at Bulette's funeral.

For several weeks after Milleain's arrest many disturbing and damning facts were brought to light against the prisoner. Bulette's house had been ransacked for money, jewelry, valuable furs, silk dresses, and many other articles of value, which began to resurface. On May 24, a Mrs. Cazentre of Gold Hill informed the authorities that she had in her possession a dress pattern that she believed had belonged to Bulette. The dress pattern was brought to Virginia City and identified by both Harry and Sam Rosener as one that they had sold to Bulette a short time before her murder. Cazentre had purchased the dress pattern from John Milleain, paying him forty dollars for it though it was worth sixty. Cazentre visited the jail and identified Milleain as the man from whom she had purchased the dress pattern. Next, a valuable diamond pin, which had been sold by Milleain to a jeweler, was identified as one seen in the possession of the murdered woman before her death.

Virginia City's chief of police located a trunk owned by John Milleain, which had been left in the care of a baker on North D Street. The trunk was taken to the police station and opened the next morning; it contained articles taken from the house of the murdered woman including some items that belonged to a Miss Annie Smith of Carson City, which she had given to Bulette for repair. Police Captain George W. Downey took the items to Carson City for identification, and Smith at once recognized them as the ones she had entrusted to the care of the murdered woman before her death.

The trunk and its contents were shown to Milleain. Realizing that he had been caught, he confessed to the murder. As reported in the *Enterprise*, he begged the lawman to "take a pistol and blow my brains out." When his request was denied, Milleain said he wanted to be hung as soon as possible.

Milleain then tried to backpedal and claim his innocence. He named Chris Blair, a man of bad character well known in Virginia City, as the murderer. Blair had been in Virginia City at the time of Bulette's murder, but had left for San Francisco on January 30, 1868. By May 30,

FROM MILLEAIN'S INMATE CASE FILE

Blair was in jail in San Francisco. He had none of the property stolen from Bulette, but it was proposed that the two men might have had a falling out when Milleain refused to share the plunder. Blair was brought to Virginia City on Sunday evening, June 2, and was seated in the jail office among several other men. Milleain was also brought into the office, and it was clear that he didn't recognize Blair. It was deduced that Milleain, in desperation upon his arrest, had randomly chosen to name Blair as the murderer based upon his bad reputation.

By June 4, Blair was released. Milleain then changed his story for the preliminary hearing and admitted that he was present when the murder was committed, but insisted that he had not taken part. Eight women then came forward to testify that they had seen Milleain in possession of Bulette's property following her death. The defendant was ordered to be held for the grand jury, and was remanded to the custody of the sheriff. Milleain prepared a detailed confession, claiming that two men, known to him only as Douglass and Dillon, had murdered Bulette while he was outside as a lookout. He wrote that he knew nothing of the murder until much later.

Milleain was indicted on June 26, and his trial commenced at 10:00 A.M. on Wednesday, July 2, 1867; testimony concluded by 4:30 P.M. At 6:30 that same evening, closing arguments began and three hours later the judge charged the jury. The jurors deliberated until nearly midnight before returning a verdict of guilty of murder in the first degree. On July 5, Milleain was sentenced to hang. After all appeals were exhausted, which took nearly eight months, the judge, on February 27, 1868, set the execution date: April 24, 1868. Efforts to have the sentence commuted to life in prison failed.

Milleain wrote another version of his confession on the eve of his execution, but it was in French, which delayed its publication in the *Enterprise*. In it he accused the sheriff of extracting the first confession by coercion and charged that the sheriff had perjured himself on the witness stand. He also accused his attorney of intentionally poor representation to ensure his conviction, and he blamed the eight women who testified, stating that the only reason they were believed was "because of their licentious looks, their popularity in the country, and their impression on all the people." He insisted that he was being hanged because he was French and the people of Virginia City did not like France or Frenchmen.

On April 25, the *Enterprise* reported on "The Execution of John Millian [*sic*] for the Murder of Julia Bulette." Mark Twain was in town on a lecture tour, and among the reporters present at the gallows. He reported that on the previous day "at 12:42 P.M. John Millian [*sic*], whose real name was Jean Marie Villain, suffered the extreme penalty of the law."

As early as 8:00 A.M. on the day of the execution, a crowd began to gather about the courthouse. Twain reported:

By 10 o'clock the sidewalks and all of B Street, for a considerable distance, was a living, swaying mass of human beings. Within another hour every window in front of the courthouse was crowded with the heads of persons eager to catch a glimpse of the prisoner when he took his seat in the carriage which was to convey him to the gallows. All awnings in the vicinity were loaded down with men and boys, and every balcony was filled with men, women and children. The crowd upon the ground crammed the stairway of the courthouse, trying to push their way into the sheriff's office—in short, poking their noses everywhere, apparently rendered recklessly stupid by their morbid curiosity.

At 11:30 A.M. the carriage for the prisoner was driven in front of the sheriff's office, and forty deputized citizens, armed with Henry rifles, surrounded the vehicle. Shortly afterward the National Guard—in full uniform and numbering sixty men—marched from their armory and tried to form a square outside of the prisoner's carriage. Spectators were closely wedged around the carriage making it impossible for it to move through the crowd. Officials scolded and pushed, but it wasn't until they ordered men to fix bayonets and load rifles with ball ammunition that the crowd cleared. There was no order to fire, but the mere act of loading unloaded rifles gave notice that they meant business. The guard then formed a lane from the door of the sheriff's office, and the prisoner, attended by Catholic priests, advanced to the carriage. Milleain walked with a quick and firm step, and the crowd, after all their trouble, caught no more than a glimpse of the condemned man as the curtains on the sides of the carriage were drawn.

At length the crowd was forced back and the procession to the gallows began at noon. A second carriage containing two physicians, who were required to attend the execution, along with members of the press, followed the carriage containing the prisoner and the priests. Immediately behind them came a hearse containing a coffin draped in black, driven by the undertaker. Deputies formed a line on either side of the carriages, and outside of their line marched the National Guard, while the policemen cleared the way in front.

The road to the gallows was lined on either side with men, women, and children, all striving to catch a glimpse of the prisoner. As far as could be seen in advance, a mob hurried along the road, over the hills and across lots and fields, in the direction of the spot chosen for the execution. It was a motley crowd, according to Twain, consisting of "white women with children in their arms; Piute squaws with young ones hanging upon their backs, pulling themselves along with broomsticks; long-tailed and wild-eyed Chinamen; Mexican women and Negro women; women of the town and women evidently from the country, with men of all kinds and colors."

The gallows had been erected in a semibasin, a little over a mile to the north of the city. Leaving the carriages on the Geiger Grade, about 150 yards above, the prisoner and his entourage marched down to the scaffold in about the same order as that observed in the carriages. The ground on three sides of the gallows rose rather abruptly, forming a sort of amphitheater, and here was a crowd of not less than three thousand persons.

The military and special deputies formed a square about the gallows, with the prisoner, priests, sheriff, two deputy sheriffs, physicians, members of the press, and a few other invited persons within. Milleain ascended the stairs leading to the scaffold with a light spring in his step, almost at a run. Upon reaching the scaffold, he turned and gazed earnestly upward at the rope, as though curious to know whether it was firmly secured to the crossbeam.

While a deputy sheriff read the death warrant, Milleain stood firmly upright and listened without the slightest tremor or change of countenance. He then turned and knelt upon the trap while the priests prayed for him. When the prayer was over, he arose. Asked by the sheriff whether he had anything to say, Milleain took from his pocket a sheet of paper upon which he had written in French. He said that he was not sufficiently conversant with the English tongue to express clearly what he wished to say. Although he wore a somewhat haggard look from his long confinement, he showed that he possessed nerves of steel as he read his lengthy manuscript in a loud, clear voice, and held the paper so firmly that not even the slightest tremor was observed. When he finished reading he spoke for another three minutes in French, then turned about and shook hands with the sheriff and kissed the priests. He stepped to the front of the scaffold and in a loud voice— and in very good English—said: ". . . I am very much obliged to you for your services and also to the kind ladies that visited me in my cell."

After Milleain kicked off his slippers, his arms and legs were pinioned, and he otherwise assisted the officers in their work. His collar was opened and the condemned man took one hasty look at the noose as it was brought forward. He stood perfectly motionless as it was being properly positioned with the knot behind his left ear, his eyes were downcast, and his lips moving as though muttering a prayer. A black cap was pulled down over his face, and on the instant that the strings were drawn tight from behind, the sheriff detached the fastenings which held the trapdoor and the body of Milleain disappeared through the opening.

The body fell six feet and the vertebrae were dislocated. After being suspended for several minutes, a tremor shook Milleain's limbs for a few seconds, and then all outward signs of vitality ceased—though his pulse persisted for nearly thirteen minutes. At the end of twenty-five minutes, Dr. Belden McMeans and Dr. C. C. Green pronounced him dead. His body was cut down, placed in the coffin, and given over to the charge of the undertakers for burial that evening at the expense of the county.

And, so, the death of their beloved "woman of the town" with the heart of gold was avenged. The lawmen were congratulated on conducting "the most stupendous hanging Nevada had ever experienced." The *Enterprise* reported that they "deserve great credit for the admirable manner in which the sad and solemn affair was conducted throughout. From the time of starting from the jail till the dead body was in the coffin there was not a single balk or halt, and best of all, there was no bungling on the scaffold—all went swift, sure and quiet. When the trap was loosened and the body fell there was a slight rush forward by the crowd, but the guards soon restored order."

Milleain did not profess his innocence nor did he resign himself to his fate as other condemned men did. Instead, he claimed that he was being hanged because he was French, a claim with no standing in a town whose population was as diverse as San Francisco or New York.

Moore and His Gang Lynched in Laramie

October 18, 1868

WITHIN A FEW SHORT WEEKS AFTER Laramie City, Wyoming, formed a government on May 1, 1868, it became clear that the gamblers and saloon owners were the ones who really ran the town. When Laramie's first elected government collapsed, Asa "Ace" Moore declared himself mayor and appointed O. S. Duggan as town marshal. Duggan in turn hired Con Weiger, Edward "Big Ed" Bernard, and "Heartless Ed" Franklin as his deputies. Together, these men were known as the "Five Bosses." To round out the slate, Moore appointed "Long" Steve Young as justice of the peace.

Moore was the proprietor of two saloons—the Diana and the Belle of the West. The latter was his operations base for criminal activity. The five bosses used their authority to recover money from those who had won at their gambling tables. They would arrest people who appeared to have any wealth or valuables worth stealing and take them into the back rooms of the Belle of the West. There, they would conduct a mock trial, pick their victim clean, and—if he seemed not to pose a threat—turn him loose; if the five bosses sensed trouble, however, they would murder him. The bodies of their victims would then be buried in unmarked graves on the prairie, or discreetly dumped in a boxcar to be found at some distant location.

In August 1868, Duggan, who was embroiled in the controversial shooting of the son of a prominent citizen, was nearly lynched by a mob led by the murdered boy's father. Duggan fled and was never seen in Laramie again. From there things quickly unraveled for Moore's gang.

In late September the good citizens of Laramie began organizing a large vigilance committee. The leaders included Tom Sears, a Civil War veteran and legitimate saloon owner; John Wright, a saddle maker; and Nathaniel K. Boswell, a member of the Rocky Mountain Detective Agency. Determined to rid their town of the lawless element, they held a people's court with the defendants *in absentia*, and then planned an organized strike for October 18, 1868, to arrest the convicted parties. The committee had compiled a list of nearly fifty undesirable individuals that they wanted to run out of town. Among the fifty, four men in Moore's gang were marked for execution, as were two other desperadoes.

At 8:00 P.M. on October 18, five hundred men gathered on the far side of the tracks behind the railroad repair shops. From there groups of men deployed to prearranged locations. At the sound of a gun fired by Sears, they were to move in and capture their assigned men from the list. The idea was to then sort them out, hanging the three main "bosses" of Moore's gang and Justice Long, and putting the rest, including the lesser criminal "Heartless Ed" Franklin, on a train out of Laramie under threat of death should they return.

However, a shot unrelated to their plan was fired, and only the party assigned to the Belle of the West was in position to make their move. The men in the Belle of the West met the attack with gunfire, and the battle lasted fifteen minutes. Con Weiger and Ed Bernard were badly wounded; Charles Barton, a coronet player, was killed;

William Willie, a fireman on Union Pacific's Engine No. 69, was shot through the bowels and expected to die; and William McPherson was shot through the leg, but expected to recover. Many others among the undesirables were wounded, and some may have died later on the train or thereafter. Asa Moore, however, avoided capture but remained in Laramie.

Weiger and Bernard were taken to an unfinished shed behind the Frontier Hotel and preparations were made to hang them. Asa Moore went to the shed and ordered the vigilantes to release Weiger and Bernard. Instead, one of the lynchers put his shotgun into Moore's belly and announced that Moore's name was on the list of six, and that he would be joining the other two. The three men had their hands tied behind them, and nooses were placed around their necks. They were hoisted up, but before they were strangled to death, their bodies were riddled with bullets. The bodies were left hanging throughout the night and into the late morning hours before being cut down.

Justice of the Peace "Long" Steve Young was captured at Lawson's Ranch, nine miles from Laramie. He was brought to town and told of the hangings. However, the committee seemed satisfied that they had done enough hanging to make their position clear, so they ordered Young to leave the city by 7:30 A.M. Young was ordered not to return under threat of death, but instead of leaving, Young went to the scene of the hangings. When he saw the bodies still suspended, he declared, according to Cheyenne's *Daily Leader*, that, "no strangling sons of b___s can drive me out of town." When he challenged anyone to take him on, several committee members stepped forward, and according to the *Leader*, they warned him to leave or they would "shoot his brains out on the spot." Young declared that he would leave, but promised to return with his friends. Young, however, still did not leave town as ordered.

Young was followed around town until 10:00 A.M. and once again he was told to leave within the hour, but again he defied the order and

LYNCHING OF LARAMIE MAYOR ASA "ACE" MOORE,
EDWARD "BIG ED" BERNARD, AND CON WEIGER

LYNCHING OF "LONG" STEVE YOUNG FROM A TELEGRAPH POLE

challenged the vigilantes. The vigilantes then seized Young and dragged him to the main railroad crossing at the foot of B Street near the depot. They selected a telegraph pole, tied his hands behind his back, put a noose over his head, and pushed him up a ladder. When lynching was imminent, Young begged for a chance to leave town, but his pleas were ignored. In the presence of hundreds of spectators, without ceremony or delay, the vigilantes pulled the rope taut, tied off the loose end, and jerked the ladder out from under Young's feet. One of the vigilantes thought Young was taking too long to die and pulled down on Young's legs, which snapped the rope. Young's body fell and while he lay sense-less on the ground, one of the men he had swindled rushed forward and kicked and stomped his head. The vigilantes pulled the angry man away, tied a new noose, and pulled Young up once more. It took but a short while for Young to strangle to death.

The committee secured a wagon and went to the shed to collect the bodies of Moore, Bernard, and Weiger. When Young was declared dead, they cut down his body. The remains of the four men were driven to a place three-quarters of a mile from the city and buried in a single wide, deep grave. En route the "women" of the dead men tried several times to pull their men off the wagon, but the vigilantes would not allow it, nor would they allow any kind of marker to be placed over the grave.

Willie and Barton died of their wounds, and on October 21, 1868, the *Leader's* editor reflected on the affairs in Laramie. He wrote:

> Without desiring to pass judgment upon those executed or their executioners in Laramie on Sunday night and Monday morning, we would ask if the sacrifice of the life of one innocent man is not too much to pay for the punishment of a dozen (presumed) guilty ones. William Willie and Charles Barton are both victims of a usurpation of the law. One, Willie, might have been engaged on the side of the Vigilantes and it may be said took his chances for what he supposed to be a public benefit or necessity; but the other, Barton, was simply a harmless musician. . . . The question is if the benefit—granted they exist—of the Laramie executioners are sufficient to justify the originators and leaders of the V. C. organization in the loss of these two men alone, supposing all the others deserved death.

Laramie's vigilante committee, which had been reduced to three hundred after the raid, was raising funds for their wounded and for the purpose of forming a permanent organization. Once the four main members of Moore's gang were executed, law was restored to Laramie, but like any settlement on the western frontier this railroad town had its share of brutal bad men and reckless desperadoes over the next five decades.

Escaped Convicts
Meet Their Fate

September 27, 1871

ON SEPTEMBER 17, 1871, THERE WAS A MASSIVE prison break at the Nevada State Prison outside Carson City. Plans for the escape were first hatched on Sunday, September 3, and for the next two weeks, breaking out was the constant topic of conversation among the inmates.

As opportunity afforded, the question of leadership was discussed among the prisoners. Jack Davis, a train robber, was considered, but several inmates objected to Davis because he had turned state's evidence at trial. J. M. Chapman and E. B. Parsons, involved in the same train robbery, were so set against Davis as a leader that they refused to participate in the break if it were to take place under his leadership. Since the cooperation of these two men was deemed essential, Davis was dropped from consideration and Leander Morton was elected as leader of the break.

Morton was convicted of robbery in Elko County and had received a thirty-year sentence on January 1, 1871. Morton and fellow prisoner Frank Clifford "worked up the case" for the break, and on Sunday, September 10, preparations commenced. The ceiling was cut away to allow access to the crawl space and a portion of the wall above was dug out. The ceiling was replaced and secured so that the guards couldn't detect the escape route.

On Sunday, September 17, the work was completed. Fourteen prisoners were posted to watch over the room of the deputy warden, and others were positioned between the ceiling and roof to pass the signal to the fourteen prisoners. When Volney R. Rollins, captain of the guard, entered the cell rooms at 6:00 P.M. to lock down for the evening, he was knocked out. Pat Hurley, serving a five-year sentence from Ormsby County, stopped the prisoners from dealing a deathblow to Rollins by dragging him into a cell.

The guards outside were unaware of the attack on Rollins and didn't know that a break was underway. The prisoners climbed to the top of the upper tier of cells and cut a passage into the quarters of Prison Warden Frank Denver. Each convict was armed with a slungshot or a crudely fashioned knife. They rushed into the warden's quarters and were met by Denver, who began firing at them to protect his wife and daughter who happened to be visiting. The prisoners overpowered and severely wounded Denver, but R. Dechman, (often misreported as Dedman) a trusty convict—proven trustworthy through model behavior—picked up a chair and fought off the attackers. Dechman was knocked senseless, and the prisoners fled down the stairs to the prison armory, where they outfitted themselves with weapons, ammunition, and some clothing. Now armed, the convicts charged out of the main building into the yard and began to fire. Nearly every guard and several prisoners received wounds, many of them quite serious. Matt Pixley, the proprietor of the nearby Warm Springs Hotel, who came when the alarm was sounded, was killed in the gunfire.

Once outside the prison walls, twenty-two of the escapees confidently marched away from the prison eastward, two went west, and five went across the railroad tracks toward Empire City. The larger party soon divided, with some men going it alone and others sectioning off

TWENTY-NINE CONVICTS ESCAPED THROUGH THE MAIN
GATE OF THE NEVADA STATE PRISON IN 1871.

into small parties. One of these parties was comprised of prison-break leader Leander Morton, Moses Black, Charles Jones, and J. B. Roberts, among others. Moses Black had been convicted of grand larceny in Nye County on September 11, 1871. J. B. Roberts had been convicted of robbery in Washoe County and sentenced to twelve years on July 20, 1871. All were desperate and dangerous men. Once they were well beyond the walls of the prison, Jones was decided upon as the best qualified to lead, since he knew best the area they were going to. He assumed command of his party and directed them toward Round Valley.

On Wednesday, September 20, four of the convicts from Jones's group passed in sight of Aurora, Nevada. It was soon learned that these four men had captured pony express rider William A. "Billy" Poor, and it was believed that he was taken hostage. A posse consisting of a deputy sheriff, Billy's brother Horace Poor, J. S. Mooney, P. Kelly, Ned Barker, John McCue, M. Lewis, and a half dozen other citizens started in pursuit. They detoured toward Mono Lake, but eventually struck the trail near Adobe Meadows. Along the trail they found one of Poor's gloves, and then the other. Next, they found the collar from his shirt. The posse followed a clear trail of Billy's very distinctive boot tracks, and was hopeful that he was still alive and could still be saved. Unfortunately, twenty-four-year-old Billy Poor had already been killed. His body was found on September 29, fifteen miles southeast of Wellington's Stage Station in Lyon County.

It was Jones who was responsible for capturing the pony express rider at gunpoint and ordering him to dismount. Morton came to assist Jones, and the two men escorted Billy two hundred yards from the road, supporting him on either side so that he walked on the heels of his boots only. Jones then ordered Billy to strip and threw him his prison shirt, which Billy pulled over his head, somewhat heartened by the fact that he was being offered clothing to keep him warm. As his head protruded through the neck hole, however, he found himself staring into the muzzle of Jones's six-shooter. In a moment, Billy was dead. Jones dressed in Billy's clothing, but finding the boots too small, gave them to Morton in exchange for his worn-down prison shoes.

Unaware of Poor's murder, the posse continued to track the convicts. Mono Jim, an Indian tracker with the posse, informed them that the convicts were encamped near Dexter's Ranch in a canyon some five miles distant. The pursuers were fatigued, however, and their animals were spent, so they did not start on the trail immediately. The deputy leading the posse then sent a note to the deputy sheriff at Hot Springs, dated September 22:

> Four or five escaped convicts from the Nevada State Prison are now concealed in the hills back of this place, and they are undoubtedly striking for Long Valley. If you can raise a posse and go there you will surely intercept them. I think they will travel tonight. We have tracked them beyond a doubt to this place. They have, I think, four animals, which must be nearly given

out. They have taken with them Billy Poor, the pony rider, for their own protection; should you go, be careful not to injure him. My men are very much fatigued and some taken sick, or I would be riding tonight. There is a reward of $500 for each, DEAD OR ALIVE. Send me an answer immediately as I expect to start early in the morning. If you think it more advisable to join me here, use your own discretion, but if you do anything, not a moment is to be lost.

As soon as the Hot Springs deputy received the news, he dispatched two men to the area and began to organize a new, refreshed posse to join the other group the following morning. The posse gathered all the firearms and ammunition they could gather and assembled at Hightower's Mill near Hot Springs. The group consisted of Deputy H. Devine, J. C. Calhoun, B. B. Alonson, James and George Dougherty, I. Nabors, James Peregrine, and three men known only as Moore, Morrison, and Nesbitt. They waited two hours for the Aurora party to join them, and while having dinner, they learned that convict Charles Jones had been to the mill the previous day to obtain bread, meat, and salt.

At 2:00 A.M., the Hot Springs posse started up the canyon. After traveling two miles, they cut the trail of the escaped convicts and followed it eighteen miles south into Long Valley, where they caught sight of the escapees. However, with night falling they went to W. J. McGee's ranch and started out again at daybreak the next morning. They headed out to the canyon and after walking and searching for several miles, they finally came upon the fugitives. A hundred yards up the canyon, one of the convicts was seen running down a hillside, so the posse immediately spurred their horses forward. Three of the fugitives quickly retreated to a large tree and dodged behind it.

As soon as the first two convicts reached the tree, they fired on the posse; the posse immediately returned fire. Four of the posse's horses were hit, killing outright those ridden by Nabors and Calhoun, and wounding the horses of Nesbitt and Alonson. Morrison was mortally wounded during this first exchange: While attempting to climb the hill to get a better position, he received a fatal wound from J. B. Roberts, and so the posse fell back to the nearby willows for shelter. Shots were exchanged for twenty minutes, until the convicts worked their way up the canyon about three hundred yards, shielded all the way by willows. At the top they stopped for a rest.

The posse following in pursuit on horseback saw Morton approach Mono Jim, the posse's Indian guide, who was holding his and the deputy's horse as instructed. The Indian stepped forward as Morton drew near, and without hesitation, Morton fired two shots from his six-shooter, killing Mono Jim.

Morton took the two horses and continued up the canyon. At that point the outgunned posse retreated to the place where the fight had first commenced and found the body of Morrison. He had been shot in the side just above the hip, the ball going entirely through his body. A second ball, the coup de grace, had entered the back of his head and passed out above the right eye. The deputy and his men buried Mono Jim on the spot and took Morrison's remains back to Benton, near Hot Springs, for burial.

A new party headed by volunteer farmers John Clarke and John Crough then started out after the murderers, going up Long Valley. This additional posse, assembled from local residents and operating independent of the first, tracked the fugitives up into a rough, precipitous canyon leading out of Round Valley into the Sierra Nevada. They pressed the escapees so hard that the convicts were compelled to shoot one tired horse, and lost another over a precipice.

From Sunday morning to Tuesday night, Clarke and Crough were without a mouthful to eat. Their Indian companions were dispatched to Round Valley several times for supplies, but without much success. Finally, word was sent that they had cornered the fugitives in a canyon, but at this place they were handicapped by the scarcity of serviceable long-range guns.

A man was dispatched at once to Camp Independence, where Major Henry C. Egbert selected five of the best men in his company and took to the field himself. He offered long arms to anyone who would accompany him, and six citizens joined his company. They traveled to Bishop's Creek in seven hours.

On Wednesday night four officers, with a Mexican guide and a party of Indian trackers, succeeded in capturing Leander Morton and Moses Black in the sand hills five miles southeast of Round Valley. There was a brief exchange of gunfire before the fugitives dropped their weapons and raised their hands. One Indian mistook this gesture for an act of aggression and fired on Black. The bullet struck him above the left temple, breaking the skull and passing out the other side, but not killing him. The fugitives, assured that there would be no further violence, surrendered. The two captured convicts were taken to a house in Round Valley and placed in custody. The prisoners disclosed that fellow escapee J. B. Roberts had been badly wounded and told the officers where he could be found.

The officers started out and pursued Roberts for two days before capturing him. They returned to Round Valley for Morton and Black, but at first could find no sign of them. After some close questioning it was learned that Black had died of his wounds, and since the ranchers at Round Valley were digging one grave, they decided they might as well dig two. Leander Morton was taken to a large tree near the gravesites and unceremoniously hanged. Both bodies were then buried, but the location of the unmarked graves was not disclosed.

Morton had been hanged because of his involvement in the murders of Pixley, Poor, Morrison, and Mono Jim, but also because, according to the *Carson (Nevada) Daily Appeal*, "the small reward would not pay for taking them to Carson and the reward was not the object of the capture." Governor L. R. Bradley's reward proclamation offered only three hundred dollars for Morton and two hundred dollars each for Black and Roberts. Once divided, it would have provided very small sums for each of the large number of men in the posse.

Roberts was returned to prison on October 20, narrowly escaping a lynching at Hot Springs. By November 15, 1871, eighteen convicts had been captured and returned to the prison, but Jones was not among them and, although a reward of one thousand dollars was offered, he would never be recaptured. The grand jury indicted those recaptured but they were all acquitted when testimony proved that only Black, Morton, and Jones were involved in the murders related to the prison break. One more convict would be captured in December 1873, but ten of the escaped prisoners were never seen nor heard of in Nevada again.

"Buffalo Curly" Assassinates "Wild Bill"

March 1, 1877

JAMES BUTLER "WILD BILL" HICKOK was no saint. He killed many men in his day and worked many of the roughest jobs in the West, including teamster, wolfer, and muleskinner. He was a hard man and some believed he deserved to die. He probably had as many enemies in Deadwood as he had friends, and John "Jack" McCall, who was using the alias Bill Sutherland in Deadwood, was prominent among the former.

John "Jack" McCall was born in Louisville, Kentucky, in 1851. When he was twenty years old, he started drifting west, taking any job he could find. In 1872 he was in Nebraska, making the rounds of the buffalo hunting camps. He earned the nickname "Buffalo Curly" or "Curly Jack" because of his naturally curly hair.

At one camp in Nebraska McCall quarreled with a man named Lee Baldwin, a candidate for the office of sheriff. McCall went after Baldwin with two six-shooters drawn, but his adversary beat him to the draw with a railroad timber. The blow not only knocked McCall unconscious for an entire day, it permanently crossed his eyes.

Using the alias Bill Sutherland, Jack McCall arrived in Deadwood, Dakota Territory, in early June 1876. He earned his money doing any job he could find and quickly spent it on liquor or lost it at cards. On August 2, just after 4:00 P.M., McCall entered the front door of the No. 10 Saloon and ordered a whiskey. A miner was having gold dust weighed at the far end of the twenty-foot bar, and McCall made his way toward the scales, near the poker table where the infamous Wild Bill was seated. He aroused no suspicion, as he would have to weigh out dust in order to join the game.

Hickok had been losing, so when William R. Massie, one of the more fortunate card players around, showed his hand, Wild Bill gave it his full attention. It was just at that moment that McCall stepped away from the bar, to within a few feet of Hickok's back. He pulled his six-shooter and sent a single, fatal ball into the brain of the legendary gunfighter. After McCall fired, he yelled, "Damn you, take that!" He continued to wave his pistol at the other patrons, most of whom vacated the saloon, and he pulled the trigger several times while pointing at those who remained, but each time the cartridge misfired. Finally he fled out the back door and up the alley behind the saloon. In a few minutes men were in pursuit, but although the murderer was seen several times, the posse could not shoot for fear of hitting innocent bystanders.

Finally McCall was cornered in a Deadwood butcher shop and captured. A mob formed and McCall was rushed down the street for a lynching. Just at that moment, however, a man rode into town with the head of an Indian; he was seeking the scalp bounty he had just earned. The lynch mob was distracted by the dead Indian, as interest was high after Custer's defeat a month earlier, but not distracted enough for McCall to escape. He was taken into custody and held for a people's court the following day.

In the morning William L. Kuykendall was elected presiding judge. The prisoner, who by then had identified himself as "Jack" McCall, was tried. He claimed, according to Chicago's *Inter-Ocean* that,

"He killed my brother so I killed him." He testified that Wild Bill Hickok killed his brother, Samuel Strawhim, in Abilene, Kansas. There was no evidence available to show that McCall was lying about his brother's murder, even though he was, so McCall was acquitted.

To avoid being killed by Wild Bill's vengeful friends, McCall fled Deadwood for Wyoming, first to Cheyenne and then to Laramie. There he began drinking heavily and bragging about killing Wild Bill Hickok while detailing how he had lied his way out of a conviction.

Deputy U.S. Marshal A. D. Balcombe overheard McCall and arrested him for murder on August 29. Following a preliminary hearing, he was taken to the Dakota Territory capital of Yankton on September 5 and indicted on October 18. On November 9, McCall tried to escape with a fellow prisoner, but after this unsuccessful attempt, he claimed he had murdered Wild Bill for money and said that he wanted to turn state's evidence. He named John Varnes, a Deadwood gambler, as the man who had hired him. When Varnes could not be found, he tried to implicate a man named Tim Brady, but Brady had also left the territory.

McCall's trial commenced on December 4 in a Yankton courtroom. No defense witnesses were called, and on December 6 at 10:15 P.M. he was finally convicted of first-degree murder.

On January 3, 1877, Judge P. C. Shannon sentenced McCall to hang on March 1, 1877. A motion for a new trial, an appeal to the Supreme Court, and a petition for commutation sent to the governor were all unsuccessful. McCall's attorneys lastly petitioned the president of the United States. When this was denied, McCall lost all hope.

Reverend Joseph Ward of the Congregationalist Church and Reverend J. A. Potter of the Methodist Episcopal Church of Yankton offered their services, but McCall declined, preferring the Catholic religion. He spent his final weeks in conversation, prayer, and bible study with Roman Catholic Father John Daxacher and his assistant J. A. Curry. He corresponded with autograph seekers, and on February 21 announced to the press that he would write an article to hand over on the morning of his execution. The article was supposed to be a confession, but he would not elaborate on the intended content.

On his final night before execution, the marshal gave McCall a letter that he had received. It read:

Merchants Hotel
Louisville, Kentucky
February 25, 1877
To the Marshal of Yankton:

Dear Sir:

I saw in the morning papers a piece about the sentence of the murderer of Wild Bill, Jack McCall. There was a young man of the name of John McCall left here about six years ago, who has not been heard from for the last three years. He has a father, mother and three sisters living here in Louisville, who are very uneasy about him since they heard about the murder of Wild Bill. If you can send us any information about him, we would be very thankful to you.

This John McCall is about twenty-five years old, has light hair, inclined to curl, and one eye crossed. I cannot say about his height, as he was not grown when he left here. Please write as soon as convenient, as we are anxious to hear from you.

Very respectfully,
Mary A. McCall

After McCall read the letter he refused to reply and would not confirm that it was from his sister. The article he had written then disappeared and was not seen again, perhaps because it would have confirmed his identity and he wanted to spare his family the humiliation of having a son executed for murder.

DEADWOOD, DAKOTA TERRITORY, DURING ITS EARLY DAYS

McCall's final morning dawned cloudy with a drizzling rain. It had been expected that McCall would break down and present a miserable display of emotion as the moment approached. In fact he maintained his composure, slept soundly his last night, and arose to eat a hearty breakfast.

McCall's irons were removed by a blacksmith during the early hours, and afterward he shaved and dressed all in black, his choice of attire, which gave him a boyish appearance. At 9:00 A.M. the prisoner was brought out of his cell by U.S. Marshal J. H. Burdick, who read the death warrant in the presence of deputies C. P. Edmunds and R. J. Stanley, Father Daxacher, and his assistant. McCall returned to his cell for a moment and upon his reemergence had a brief, whispered conversation with Father Daxacher. Outside a large crowd had braved the light rain for a glimpse of the condemned man. At 9:30 McCall bade farewell to his fellow prisoners and left the jail for the last time.

DEADWOOD, DAKOTA TERRITORY, IN AUGUST 1876

The procession to the gallows included L. D. F. Poore, representing the *New York Herald*; Mr. Bryant of the *New England Journal*; Dr. Wilson and the Taylor brothers of the *Dakota Herald*; and Phil K. Faulk of the *Daily Press and Dakotian*. Father Daxacher and assistant Curry, special guard General D. Mathieson, Marshal Burdick, and Deputies Edmunds, Stanley, and H. C. Ash accompanied the prisoner. Burdick and Ash used a light carriage to lead the way; behind them was another carriage with the prisoner, clergy, Edmunds, and local reporter Faulk. The remainder of the men followed by whatever means they had arranged, and there was a long line of carriages and wagons in advance and behind the marshal's procession. Not a word was spoken during the two-mile ride to the school section, north of town and just beyond the Catholic cemetery. They arrived at the gallows at 10:00 A.M.

The gallows had a framework measuring eight feet by ten feet, and the platform on which the trap was arranged stood eight feet from the ground. The entire structure, from two feet above the platform to the

JAMES BUTLER "WILD BILL" HICKOK, JOHN MCCALL'S VICTIM

ground, was closely boarded up so that it was impossible to observe the last death struggle of the condemned man. A deputy sheriff and a deputy U.S. marshal shared responsibility for crowd control and had done so well that there was no crowding or unseemly conduct at the gallows.

As soon as his carriage arrived, McCall stepped down and was escorted to the platform by Deputy Ash. He took his place in the center of the trapdoor and, gazing eastward, examined the throng of over one thousand curious spectators. Only the marshal, Deputy Ash, and the clergy were allowed on the platform. McCall's limbs were bound, but he managed to kneel and pray with his priest. He turned his face skyward and kissed the crucifix when it was offered; it was placed in his right hand and he clenched it tightly. He then stood up and a black cap was pulled over his face. Marshal Burdick arranged the noose, but McCall said, "Wait one moment, Marshal, until I pray." The marshal paused and when the prayer concluded, McCall said, "Draw it tighter, Marshal." Burdick complied

At 10:15 A.M. the trap was sprung just as the condemned man uttered, "Oh, God!" The prisoner dropped four feet, breaking his neck. Twelve minutes after the trapdoor opened, Drs. D. F. Etter and J. M. Miller were admitted to the enclosure beneath the gallows to pronounce the death. They reported that McCall's head drooped toward his breast, "his hands were clenched and blue," and the crucifix was still clutched tightly in his right fist. They examined the body for a pulse and found none. Reporter Phil Faulk noted, "After hanging ten minutes longer, the body was cut down and placed in a neat walnut coffin." McCall's remains were removed to the southwest corner of the Catholic cemetery and buried following a brief ceremony by Father Daxacher.

At his trial McCall did not present the same defense he had used successfully in Deadwood—that Wild Bill had killed his brother—perhaps because by now it was well known that he had no brother, dead or alive. However, it was certain that McCall had murdered Wild Bill over money and an imagined insult. Despite his reasons, this simple man was responsible for killing one of the old West's most notorious characters.

John D. Lee
Pays for the Mountain
Meadows Massacre

March 23, 1877

IN 1844 JOHN D. LEE WAS SELECTED as a member of a forty-man police force in the Mormon city of Nauvoo, Illinois. The *Danites* or "Destroying Angles" as they were called had the responsibility of keeping order in the city, but their primary function was guarding the Prophet—the man leading the Mormon Church—and his disciples. Often Danites would be called upon to perform a duty such as a burglary, robbery, or murder, and anyone who threatened the life of a church leader was marked for death. When a certain job was assigned to a Danite, he was prohibited from questioning its justice or legality. The men were brainwashed to believe that they would not be blamed for whatever acts they committed and that the leaders would bear the responsibility.

When the Mormons moved west to Utah Territory, the Prophet continued to use his force of Danites to carry out crimes and killings in his name—supposedly for a higher power. While the practice focused on gentiles, Mormons who consorted with non-Mormons or offended church leaders were also marked for death. Lee was among those who moved to Utah. In 1850 he made his home in Parowan, Iron County, where over the next seven years he helped to build up the town. He continued to be faithful to the Prophet even when years later it seemed the Mormon leaders had abandoned and sacrificed him to the authorities.

In August 1857 a California-bound wagon train of some 140 Methodist emigrants from Boone County, Arkansas, led by Captain John T. Baker and Captain Alexander Fancher, paused at Salt Lake City to restock. They were not well received and could not obtain provisions, so they swung south, stopping at each Mormon settlement for the same purpose—but with the same results.

While pausing at these settlements, Fancher was overheard making loud threats. The Mormons' reluctance to help the emigrant party turned to open hostility. Fancher declared that once the train was in California, he would muster an army and return to punish the Mormons.

On September 5, 1857, the wagon train reached Mountain Meadows in the southwest part of Utah Territory, and camped. At daybreak on September 7, Paiute Indians attacked the camp, murdering and mutilating twenty adult members of the party, and driving off the stock. Fancher appealed to the Mormons for aid, and John D. Lee, accompanied by a regiment of Parowan's military and Paiute Indian auxiliaries, agreed to escort the emigrants the fifty miles to Cedar City. They required, however, that Fancher and his men first surrender their arms. The emigrant party, almost out of ammunition, agreed and loaded their wagons to leave Mountain Meadows. They had not gone more than a few hundred yards when the Mormons and the party of Paiute Indians turned on the emigrants, murdering and mutilating all who were old enough to one day testify against them, sparing only seventeen children under eight years of age.

One incident in particular characterized the savage and bloodthirsty nature of the attack. In the middle of the melee, two young sisters escaped together and concealed themselves in a thicket, until an Indian chief discovered and captured them. A boy was dispatched to bring Lee, and the girls were trembling as the chief asked Lee what he should do with them. Lee said, "They are too old to live," and the Indian responded, "They are too pretty to kill." At this moment the older of the two girls threw herself on Lee's breast, wound her arms about his neck, and said:

> Oh, Sir, for God's sake, for your mother's, for your wife's, for your sister's sake, please let us live! Don't kill us; I can't bear to die. Oh, Sir, I'm too young to be put to death so cruelly! If you will let me live I promise to be your faithful servant; to tend upon you, to see to all your wants, to be everything you could wish a poor girl to be, all your life long. And poor Ella, sir, she is younger than I. For the love of the Saviour, don't let the Indian do her harm. Please, Sir, as you hope to rest beyond the grave, let us have our lives.

The Indian, not understanding a word that was said, again asked Lee, "What shall we do with them?" Lee looked down at the girl whose arms were wrapped around his neck and said, "It is beyond my power to save you. I am acting under orders." At this the younger girl pulled her sunbonnet down over her eyes and the Indian chief, overawed by Lee's charisma, took aim and shot her in the forehead, killing her instantly. At the same moment Lee untwisted the older girl's arms from his neck, grabbed her hair, drew her head back across his breast, and cut her throat from ear to ear with his hunting knife.

The massacre was accepted as part of the Prophet's plan, and no one was punished. Soon after the massacre, Lee was elected to the Utah legislature and moved to Salt Lake City, where he lived very well. However, in 1874, the national political atmosphere changed and it was decided that someone must pay for the Mountain Meadows outrage. Lee was arrested by a deputy U.S. marshal. He was indicted for the murders of the emigrants, convicted at trial in July 1875, and sentenced to be shot. The usual appeals were filed, which stayed the execution. Lee was

JOHN DOYLE LEE, LEADER OF THE
MOUNTAIN MEADOWS MASSACRE

confident that Brigham Young, leader of the Mormon Church, would at some point intervene and save his life. Over the next two years, Lee made at least four confessions, but never implicated the church elders in the massacre. All efforts to obtain a new trial or a commutation of sentence failed. Young never came forward in defense of Lee.

Ironically, the place chosen for Lee's execution was the site of the Mountain Meadows Massacre, where a monument to the event had been erected. Since a portion of the road was over very uneven terrain, it took nearly thirty hours to make the trip. A U.S. marshal had made all the arrangements for the execution and kept the site secret except to the few officials acting as witnesses and to the newspaper reporters. Lee was taken from his cell at Fort Cameron on Wednesday afternoon, placed in a covered carriage, and driven southward. A company of soldiers formed an escort for the prisoner and officials to prevent any rescue attempts. Shortly after Lee's caravan departed, three other wagons left Beaver with instructions to arrive at the monument by 10:00 on the morning of March 23. Lee was silent during the entire trip. His group arrived a mile from the monument at 8:00 P.M. on the day before the scheduled execution and made camp.

The next morning Lee broke his silence and talked freely with anyone interested. He talked of the massacre and admitted to personally killing five people, but would not reveal their sex or age. As the hour of his execution drew near, he recanted his confession and again professed his innocence.

At 10:30 A.M. Lee's coffin was placed one hundred yards east of the monument, about twenty-five feet in front of a corral formed by three government wagons drawn into a semicircle. The wagons were covered by blankets, and behind the blankets stood nine men armed with rifles. The spectators were kept on the west side of a ravine to prohibit them from identifying the executioners. As soon as everything was in place, Lee was brought forward, leaning on the arm of his religious advisor from Beaver. He was placed on the end of his coffin.

LEE, SEATED ON HIS COFFIN, BEFORE BEING LEGALLY
EXECUTED BY RIFLE FIRE

At 10:34 A.M. the U.S. marshal read the execution order from the district court and asked Lee if he had anything to say to the small crowd of witnesses. Lee stood and said he was not afraid to die. Lee, now disillusioned and discouraged, said, "I believe in the mercy of God, but I also believed that Brigham Young is leading the people astray while the doctrine of the Church leads to salvation." He concluded, "I did everything in my power to save [the emigrants], but I am the one that must suffer . . . I ask the Lord my God to extend his mercy to me and receive my spirit. My labors are done." He then asked the executioners to spare his limbs and hit his heart.

A photographer set up his equipment and photographed the scene, after which Lee asked that copies of the photograph be sent to his three wives. Pastor Stokes next offered a prayer, and Lee knelt by his coffin. The marshal then tied a handkerchief over Lee's eyes, but left his arms unbound—at the prisoner's request—and directed him to place his hands on his head. The marshal stepped back a few paces and at exactly 11:00 A.M. gave the command: "Ready! Aim! Fire!"

Nine rifles discharged almost simultaneously. Lee dropped back upon his coffin, instantly dead. An examination showed that three rifle balls had pierced his heart, one ball had struck his sternum, and the fifth ball had struck his shoulder; the other four rifles had been loaded with powder only. The body was placed in the coffin and tipped up for another photograph. Lee's remains were loaded into a wagon and taken to Cedar City in southwestern Utah, then forwarded to Panguitch, Utah, for delivery to his family.

In 1859 the Army constructed the first monument erected at the remote site of the Mountain Meadows Massacre, and over the years it deteriorated until it was a crumbling mass of rocks by 1877. It was replaced several times over the next 125 years, and a new memorial was built as the twenty-first century approached. This concrete edifice contains the names of those believed to have been killed during the massacre and buried nearby. The inscription reads, "In the valley below, between September 7 and 11, 1857, a company of more than 120 Arkansas emigrants led by Capt. John T. Baker and Capt. Alexander Fancher was attacked while en route to California. This event is known as the Mountain Meadows Massacre."

The Pickled Parrott

March 22, 1881

"BIG NOSE" GEORGE PARROTT WAS one of Wyoming's most active criminals in the late 1870s. When he tried to wreck a train with the intent of robbing it—the first such attempt in the West—an alert crew prevented the derailing. He killed two lawmen on his trail and eluded arrest for several years, but was eventually captured. Before he could be tried for murder, however, he was lynched in Rawlins, Wyoming. His place in history was secured when he was skinned and a pair of shoes was made from the resulting human leather. The rest of Parrott was pickled.

On August 19, 1878, "Big Nose" George Parrott—by birth George Francis Warden—assembled his men for an assault on Union Pacific's westbound No. 3 train near Medicine Bow, Wyoming. Parrott's gang consisted of "Dutch" Charley Bates, Jack Campbell, Joe Minuse, Tom Reed, Frank Towle, Sim Wann, and John Wells. Together, these eight men loosened a rail near Medicine Bow with the intent of wrecking and robbing the train. An alert section foreman, however, discovered the loosened rail and warned the engineer and authorities, then repaired the rail before the next train passed.

The Parrott gang, seeing their plan foiled and knowing a posse would soon be on their trail, fled toward Elk Mountain and found a hiding place among the cedars in Rattlesnake Canyon, where they waited to ambush the posse. Soon Deputy Sheriff Robert Widdowfield and Tip Vincent, a Union Pacific agent, came within rifle range of the robbers. As soon as the lawmen were in their sights, Bates opened up on Widdowfield, killing him instantly, while Parrott took careful aim, killing Vincent. Needing food, supplies, and money to make their escape, the gang next robbed the Trabing Mercantile on Crazy Woman Creek. Parrott, who liked his liquor, also stole two barrels of whiskey and a horse to pack it on.

The gang fled north into Montana and hid out for some time among a group of unsuspecting trappers on the Musselshell, where Parrott arranged to trade some of the whiskey to the local Indians in exchange for stolen horses. The gang drove the horses north and sold them in Canada, then stole a herd north of the border and drove them south to sell at Fort Benton.

In early December 1878, a man from Fort Benton visited Rawlins and told of a big-nosed man named George Reynolds, an alias for Parrott, who had been bragging of his exploits. Several of Rawlins's best men were immediately dispatched to Fort Benton, but Parrott was long gone by then. Locals at Fort Benton repeated several of George's stories to the men from Rawlins, including the details of how George and his men had planned to derail the No. 3 train and rob it—and how Widdowfield and Vincent had been murdered at the hands of George and "Dutch" Charley when their plan went sour.

Descriptions of "Big Nose" George and "Dutch" Charley were circulated. In late December 1878 "Dutch" Charley was arrested at the Pioneer Hotel in Green River by Albany County Deputy Sheriff John LaFever; Parrott remained on the run. After a short stay in the jail at Laramie City, Wyoming, "Dutch" Charley was placed on a train to Rawlins for a trial, but he never made it farther than Carbon City.

On January 5, 1879, "Dutch" Charley was aboard passenger train No. 3, the same train the Parrott gang had planned to wreck in

"BIG NOSE" GEORGE PARROTT

August 1878. It stopped at Carbon City at 9:25 P.M. A party of masked men boarded the train, overpowered officer Ed Kern, and took "Dutch" Charley from the lawman. Without ceremony or delay, they marched him to a telegraph pole adjacent to the station and threw a rope over a crossbar. The noose end was fastened about the criminal's neck, and the only delay came when the masked men allowed him to confess to the killing of Widdowfield and detail Parrott's killing of Vincent. "Dutch" Charley begged them to shoot him to death rather than hang him, but he was hoisted up and allowed to slowly strangle to death.

The reward for the capture of Parrott, the known murderer of Vincent, had grown to two thousand dollars. He had no choice but to hide out. However, as his funds dwindled and his courage increased with each passing day, he surfaced again along the stage route between Miles City, Montana, and Deadwood, Dakota Territory. Much of his old gang had joined him and, fully masked and using scatterguns similar to those carried by Wells, Fargo & Company messengers, pulled several hold-ups before a particularly lucrative venture in July 1880. Parrott obtained so much loot from New Yorker Isaac Katz that he decided to retire from the road agent business for a short while.

Parrott frequently patronized a Miles City saloon, where he enjoyed spending his ill-gotten loot and bragging to one of the girls there. She retold Parrott's tales to others who patronized the saloon and word soon reached Rawlins and Sheriff Robert Rankin. Parrott's big mouth and bragging got him in trouble again. The sheriff and a deputy set out on their way to Miles City within hours to capture him. Parrott was arrested in Miles City without a struggle and taken by train toward Rawlins before the Miles City lawmen could stop the transfer, in the event that they might want to prosecute the prisoner there before allowing him to leave the state.

On August 7, 1880, at Carbon City, twenty masked men boarded Parrott's train and took the prisoner from the lawmen. They escorted him onto the station platform, put a noose around his neck, yanked him up, and then lowered him and asked for a full confession. When he hesitated the men pulled him up several times and then promised that if he confessed, he would be given a fair trial—but if he did not confess, he would be hung. Parrott talked, and once he began, he gave every detail of his various criminal ventures, some of which were quite a surprise to the vigilantes. The mob, true to their word, then returned the prisoner to the custody of Sheriff Rankin.

Parrott was tried during the fall 1880 term of the district court in Rawlins. He was found guilty of the murder of Tip Vincent, and in mid-December was sentenced to hang on April 2, 1881. The condemned man seemed to sit quietly in his cell awaiting his end, but all the while he was planning an escape.

On March 20, 1881, he made his move. At 7:30 that night, Sheriff Rankin entered the jail corridor to lock down the prisoners. Parrott had managed to remove his heavy, homemade iron shackles. He used them as a weapon, striking Rankin on the head numerous times and knocking him semiconscious. Mrs. Rankin heard the scuffle and rushed to the jail to lock the door to the cells, her husband still inside with the prisoners. She then grabbed a revolver and stood guard at the door, while her sister ran downtown to sound the alarm. A force of men immediately came to Sheriff Rankin's rescue, and Parrott was locked in his cell, as were the other prisoners. Extra guards were placed in the jail.

Sheriff Rankin asked the townsmen to wait the short time remaining before the prisoner was to be legally hanged, but the general opinion was that the sheriff had taken enough abuse from the prisoner and that Parrott might yet escape if left to await his fate on April 2. On March 22 at 10:55 P.M., a party of thirty masked men went to the jail and removed Parrott. They marched him to a telegraph pole in front of the J. W. Hugus Company store on Main Street, opposite the railroad machine shops. A rope was placed over the crossbeam of a telegraph pole, the noose was secured around the prisoner's neck, and Parrott was forced

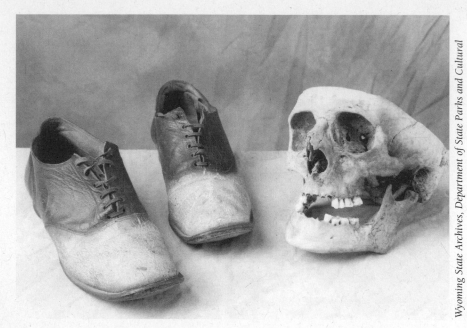

PARROTT'S SKULL AND THE SHOES MADE FROM HIS SKIN

to stand upon a barrel. Parrott begged piteously to be shot and cried out that it was cruel to hang him, but his pleas were ignored. When the barrel was kicked out, the rope and his neck stretched sufficiently that his feet did not clear the ground. He was taken down and a ladder was brought over. After being coaxed and pushed up the ladder to an acceptable height, the noose was again placed around his neck. His last words were, "I will jump off, boys, and break my neck." The crowd was not sympathetic to his wishes for a speedy, painless death and the ladder was pulled away. Without a drop, he dangled for some time as he slowly strangled to death.

Mutilation of a dead body was not an altogether uncommon occurrence in the annals of frontier justice. After hanging for a day, the body of Parrott was cut down by Thomas Maghee, William Daley, and

PARROTT'S REMAINS, UNEARTHED IN 1950, IN THE
WHISKEY BARREL IN WHICH HE WAS PICKLED

Coroner A. G. Edgerton, who took the remains to Daley's Undertaking Parlor. Assisted by Dr. John E. Osborne, Edgerton conducted an autopsy.

After the examination was complete, Dr. Osborne made a plaster of paris death mask, cut a large skin sample from the chest area, and kept the skullcap, which had been removed to examine the brain. The rest of Parrott's remains were placed in a whiskey barrel filled with a saline solution, effectively pickling the body. It was buried in an unmarked grave without ceremony. Later Dr. Osborne tanned the chest skin and sent the human leather to a shoemaker, requesting that each shoe be made so that a nipple appeared at the tips. The skinning had not been done properly, however, so when the shoes arrived, there were no nipples as had been requested. The doctor still wore the shoes on special occasions and when elected Governor of Wyoming, he wore the shoes to his inaugural ball. The skullcap was given to Osborne's assistant, Dr. Lillian Heath, who used it as a doorstop.

In 1950 the whiskey barrel was dug up during a construction project. After some curiosity and confusion, Parrott was identified by fitting the skullcap, which was still in the possession of Dr. Heath, to the remainder of the skull. The skullcap and the shoes made of human skin are now on display at the Carbon County Museum in Rawlins.

The Pond Brothers
Lynched by Vigilantes

May 23, 1881

ARTHUR POND LEFT HIS FATHER'S FARM in West Liberty, Iowa, in the summer of 1880 and went to Colorado to look for a job. He found work as a miner, but soon obtained a job as a tracklayer with the Denver & Rio Grande Railroad at Silver Cliff. The railroad provided him with a ticket to Silver Cliff, and on the train he met William "Old Bill" Miner, a California stagecoach robber passing himself off as "California Bill." Miner had been released from San Quentin Prison just a few weeks earlier on July 14, 1880.

Miner had a peculiar talent for finding men who were desperate and willing, and he sized up Pond as just such a man. He dazzled Pond with tales of thrilling robberies and huge plunder, and convinced the youngster that they could not be tracked or arrested. Pond left the train at Cañon City to join California Bill in a life of crime. They bought pistols—Pond preferring a .38 caliber British Bulldog—and then walked to Alpine, inconspicuous among the many miners who walked everywhere in those parts of Colorado.

Pond soon adopted the sobriquet "Billy Le Roy," the name by which he would be known from that time on, and on September 23 at

10:00 P.M., the duo stopped the stagecoach between Alpine and Gunnison. Unfortunately for Pond and Miner, they only found fifty dollars aboard. Still looking for a large haul, they stopped the stagecoach between Lake City and Slum Gullion Pass on October 7, and this time found one hundred dollars aboard.

Having doubled their take, they saw better hauls ahead and went into the San Luis Valley. There, on October 14, they stopped the stagecoach traveling from Alamosa to Del Norte, and this time captured nearly four thousand dollars. The two road agents went to Pueblo and divided the money. Miner became upset over Le Roy's usurpation of leadership, and they agreed to dissolve their partnership and went their separate ways. Le Roy never saw Miner again. He was now a wanted man and went east to Chicago spending his share of the loot before returning to Denver by early January.

At 6:30 on the evening of January 14, 1881, Le Roy was recognized and arrested by postal inspector Robert A. Cameron and Deputy U.S. Marshal Sim W. Cantril. The lawmen found his .38 caliber British Bulldog pistol on him, and he was lodged in jail. Le Roy was taken before U.S. Commissioner Andrew H. Brazee on two counts of stagecoach robbery and held on seven thousand dollars bail to await action by the grand jury. He then gave a detailed confession of his Colorado exploits to Cameron.

On October 26, Le Roy led an attempt to escape, with prisoners J. C. Johnson, James D. Stout, and Harry Proctor taking part. Le Roy struck guard Terry Owens over the head with a heavy padlock, but the officer was not knocked unconscious and was able to call for help. Guard G. B. Patterson and the jailer responded, and when the guard shot Johnson and Proctor, all the prisoners surrendered immediately. The following day Le Roy was taken into court on the third charge of stagecoach robbery, the first two charges set aside in favor of the one with the most damning evidence, and he was held on five thousand dollars bail. He was indicted, convicted, and on February 28, he was sentenced to serve ten years at the House of Corrections in Detroit, Michigan.

A month later Le Roy was cuffed, shackled, and put aboard a Kansas & Pacific train, with Cantril and Patterson guarding him. As the train neared Hays City, Kansas, Cantril, seeing Patterson and Le Roy asleep, went to the washroom. He was only inside a minute when he heard a commotion and found that his prisoner had escaped.

Cantril went into Hays City and then to the nearby fort for assistance, but the soldiers were reluctant to take the field. He finally offered an irresistible incentive—he would provide all manner of delicacies for the troopers meals while they were on Le Roy's trail. Although Cantril nearly went bankrupt in keeping his word, the men never caught a glimpse of the fugitive. Cantril posted his own reward of two hundred dollars for the capture of Le Roy, but it was never paid. U.S. Marshal Philip P. Wilcox decided to use postcard flyers to broadcast the information on Le Roy as there were so many wanted posters being distributed that they were lost among the pile on every lawman's desk. The postcards also proved ineffective, however, and were not used again in Colorado for that purpose.

Le Roy went to his father's farm and obtained the sum of $17.50, all the money his father had. He recruited his brother Silas, telling him of the big haul he and "Old Bill" had taken in the San Luis Valley. Silas, who adopted the alias "Sam Potter," and the Pond brothers returned quietly to Denver in early May. There, they recruited a middle-aged transient who gave his name as Frank Clark.

On the night of May 13, 1881, the eastbound stagecoach from Denver was at a point fifteen miles below Del Norte when the three road agents stepped out of the darkness and tried to stop the coach. Their sudden appearance startled the team, and the driver, Jack Wells, took advantage of the situation and whipped up the horses, steering the stagecoach out of danger under a hail of bullets. With no one injured and nothing stolen, the robbers were not pursued.

At 9:00 on Wednesday evening, May 18, the same three men stepped onto the road six miles east of Clear Creek. They immediately fired shots at driver Joe McCormick and passenger Frank Bartlett, a civil engineer with the Denver & Rio Grande Railroad. Frank Clark aimed his rifle and put a bullet through the right thigh of Bartlett, but the Pond brothers fired their pistols wide of the mark, perhaps missing on purpose. Clark's rifle bullet passed through Bartlett's leg, through the coach, and barely missed the heads of passengers William Lawrence and J. H. Lancaster. Le Roy climbed aboard the coach, stuck his pistol in Bartlett's face, announced he was looking for "sugar," and took a gold watch and $118 from Bartlett. McCormick had nothing to contribute but his pistol, and as he reached for it Le Roy said, "Never mind, keep your hands up, I will wait upon myself." Once Le Roy was finished, Clark went to the rear boot or storage area and removed five bags of mail. They ordered the coach to continue on, leaving the inside passengers unmolested. McCormick turned the coach around and drove back to Clear Creek Station.

Word of the robbery was dispatched to Del Norte, where the outraged citizens contributed a nine-hundred-dollar reward. The Denver & Rio Grande Railway posted an additional five-hundred-dollar reward. However, by the time a posse was assembled and reached the scene of the robbery, three inches of snow had fallen, obliterating all the tracks. The posse spread out and began circling, increasing the search with each pass, until the mailbags were found a mile from the road. It was later learned that the mail had contained $1,286.57 in bank drafts and $45.00 cash.

The robbers, not familiar with the terrain, avoided the rough country and followed the roads. They came to the North Clear Creek camp of William H. Cochran (sometimes spelled Cochrane), who led a surveying party, and here the fugitives ate breakfast. However, their suspicious behavior alerted Cochran that something was amiss, so he sent a man to Clear Creek Station to learn of any news in the area.

Word was sent to the posse, and four men proceeded directly to the surveyor's camp, where they cut the trail of the suspicious men. They were joined by Lew Armstrong, J. P. Galloway, Max G. Frost, and Dan Soward. After traveling only two miles, the eight-man posse came upon a man holding a rifle, and he fit the description of one of the robbers. They captured him without a fight and he readily admitted to being in on the robbery two days earlier and firing shots at stagecoach driver Jack Wells a week earlier. He gave his name as Sam Potter and talked freely, saying that one of his "pards" had gone into Lake City for supplies while the other, whom he identified as his brother Billy Le Roy, had gone to a nearby camp to buy supplies and a rifle. Armstrong sent the prisoner to Clear Creek Station with Frost and Soward while the rest of the posse camped a distance away. Armstrong and Galloway hid near the camp to await the return of the other two robbers.

They only had to wait an hour before Le Roy appeared and dismounted one hundred twenty yards distant. The lawmen stepped out of the brush and ordered him to surrender, but instead Le Roy pulled his pistol and prepared to make a stand. When he saw that he was covered with rifles from beyond the range of his pistol, he turned and ran for a willow thicket, but Armstrong shot him in the left leg and he had to surrender. Le Roy said, "I wish you had killed me. The jig is up now, and I will be done for. I am already sentenced to ten years at the House of Corrections in Detroit, and they will wind me up."

Armstrong asked, "Why? Who are you?" and their prisoner replied, "I am Billy Le Roy, the road agent and desperado." They took from him a .38 caliber British Bulldog revolver, a rather small weapon for a road agent, and almost identical to the pistol he had carried in Denver in January. When questioned about the use of such a small caliber weapon he said, "a corn cob is just as good as a pistol to hold up a coach with."

Le Roy was taken to Clear Creek Station and searched, and the lawmen found all the stolen bank drafts in his pockets. Le Roy, who bragged that he was the greatest road agent in Colorado at the time, said he had given the rest of the loot from the stagecoach robbery to Clark. Frost and Galloway went back to the robbers' camp to await his arrival. However, Clark never returned and was not heard of again.

Less than a week after robbing the stagecoach the Pond brothers were rejoined and loaded onto a wagon and taken to the Wagon Wheel Gap stage station. John Murphy, the proprietor of the station, had received word that over two hundred citizens were awaiting the prisoners, and it was feared that they were planning a "lynchin' bee,"—to take the prisoners from the law and suspend them from a limb. Armstrong decided that the posse and prisoners would take their time in order to arrive at Del Norte at a late hour to avoid the crowd. They stopped at the ranch of Edwin Shaw for a change of horses and delayed there while Mrs. Rebecca Shaw dressed Le Roy's wound and generally fawned over the brothers. The party then went on to Piños Creek, west of Del Norte, where they waited for darkness. Here the boys talked freely and at one point pleaded for pistols, Le Roy saying, "I would not mind being killed if I could have a chance to fight, but this thing of being taken out by a mob and strangled is bad."

After the sun had set several of the posse men scouted out a safe route into town and soon had their prisoners safely lodged in the jail at Del Norte. Armstrong assigned Willard Cleghorn, George Sieberd, and John Ewing to the first watch, and also assigned three more men to stand a second watch. He took the keys to the cells with him and went home. The first watch was to be relieved at midnight, at which time Armstrong intended joining the guards at the jail.

Meanwhile, the town's angry citizens organized a People's Committee for Safety. Before midnight this vigilante group overpowered Armstrong at his home, bound his wrists and ankles, left a guard to watch over the lawman, and took from him the keys to the jail cells. Shortly after midnight there was a knock at the jail door and, when the guard asked who it was, the visitor replied, "Lew," meaning Armstrong.

THE POND BROTHERS,
PROPPED UP AFTER THEIR HANGING.

The door was opened and a mob of forty armed, masked men rushed in and took the guards prisoner. The vigilantes went to the cells and accosted the Pond brothers. Before they were gagged, Le Roy barked, "You Goddamn sons of b____s."

A wagon was driven up to the door of the jail and the boys, with wrists bound, were loaded onto the wagon's bed among a half dozen armed men. The party stopped beneath a large cottonwood tree, not far from the railroad tracks, where a stout limb could support two bodies. The brothers were taken out of the wagon as ropes were being thrown over the limb, and the nooses were placed about the neck of each boy and cinched tight. The gags were then removed and the boys were asked if they had anything to say. They declined and, while they stood beneath that limb contemplating what they might say to save themselves, their legs were bound. Before they could think of anything to declare they were drawn up at the same time. A note was pinned to the chest of Le Roy which said, "Road Agents, Bunko Steerers, and Horse-thieves BEWARE!"

After their lives were extinct the brothers were cut down and returned to the jail where they remained until the next morning. Dr. L. T. Holland, the county Coroner, summoned a jury of six men and they found, "said persons above named [the Pond brothers] and described, came to their death by hanging, at the hands of disguised men. . . . the jury are unable to identify from the evidence or otherwise."

Following the inquest, photographer J. J. Cornish was allowed to take the bodies, which were "stiff as steel bars" from rigor mortis, and prop them against the outside jail wall. He took their picture and later sold copies with the caption, "Adios, Pond Bros.—road agents." The bodies were then taken to the town's cemetery and buried in an obscure corner in plot 45A.

It was not uncommon for citizens to take matters into their own hands when they were outraged, or when they lost confidence in their lawmen or the courts. That's exactly what happened in the case of the Pond Brothers—vigilantes made sure they paid for their crimes.

Gilbert and Rosengrants Hanged by Double "Twitch-Up" Gallows

July 29, 1881

MURDERERS FRANCIS GILBERT AND Merrick Rosengrants were sentenced to die on the same day on the same gallows near Denver, Colorado. Because this was a double hanging, a special apparatus with separate weights for each man called the "twitch-up" gallows had been prepared for the event. Thousands came to see the two murderers "jerked to Jesus!" using this unique apparatus.

Francis Gilbert wasn't always a criminal. An only child, he was born in New York on December 9, 1851. He was raised on a farm and attended school for five years. When he reached a proper age, he went to work in a malt house in Utica, New York, and after a time he managed the shop. He stayed only two years before moving to a factory in New York City, where he worked at a series of different occupations, always doing well. In 1878 he moved to Leadville, Colorado, where he worked as a freighter for two years. In early 1880, he moved seven miles away to the coal pits at Tennessee Park to learn the charcoal business. In a short time Gilbert and a documented coworker acquired several pits.

In September 1880 a man named Connors went to the coal pits and arranged for the delivery of a large quantity of charcoal, which he was going to resell in smaller lots. The arrangement was that Connors would pay Gilbert the day after he received payment for the charcoal he resold, which was supposed to be on October 1. Connors sent James McCullom and his assistant to haul the charcoal and get vouchers, or weight checks, for the amount hauled away. The vouchers were given to Connors so that he could make payment, although late, on October 2. But when the day for payment arrived, Connors defaulted.

On October 3, Gilbert and a promising young attorney named Thomas A. Hendricks went into Leadville to look for Connors and McCullom. Their search took them into the saloons. The men were no where to be found, so Gilbert and Hendricks decided to have a drink; they were soon inebriated. Gilbert brandished his revolver on the streets of Leadville, loudly swearing vengeance upon the two men whom he believed had swindled him.

Unable to find either man, Gilbert and Hendricks started back for Tennessee Park at dusk. They stopped at the saloon at the head of Tennessee Park and asked the barkeep if he knew the whereabouts of Connors and McCullom. The barkeep said he didn't know, and Gilbert replied, "Somebody is going to die." Gilbert and Hendricks soon learned from someone in the saloon of the location of McCullom's cabin, about three-quarters of a mile from the saloon, and made their way there.

When they arrived at the cabin, Gilbert pounded on the door. Of the several men living in the cabin one of them answered the knock. When asked about Connors, the man said he was not there. Gilbert could see through the half-opened door, however, and recognized McCullom who was seated on a stool in the middle of the cabin. Gilbert addressed the man again and said, "Never mind, this man will do just as well. He's one of the sons of b___s who are trying to swindle me out of my money."

Gilbert pushed his way into the cabin, demanding his money. McCullom said he knew nothing of the matter, which only served to infuriate Gilbert further. Gilbert pulled out his six-shooter and fired at McCullom, but missed. McCullom jumped up and grabbed the gun barrel, and as they struggled, Gilbert suddenly let go of his grip with his left hand, drew a large Bowie knife, and plunged it into McCullom's back. The next thrust of the knife cut into McCullom's arm and a third penetrated his right side. The wounded man drew his revolver as he staggered out of the cabin door, with Gilbert following closely. Gilbert recovered his six-shooter and fired again. The ball penetrated McCullom's shoulder, and McCullom returned fire but missed. Gilbert's third shot went entirely through his victim's body. McCullom staggered around the corner of the cabin and disappeared into the dark brush.

Gilbert returned to the cabin and threatened the man who had answered the door as well as another teamster. He waved his gun back and forth at the men and ordered, "Go out and look for him; I want to see whether the damned son of a b___ is dead; if he ain't I want to kill him." Gilbert followed them out and Hendricks joined in the search, but they could not find McCullom, so Gilbert and Hendricks left.

Concerned about McCollum, one of the men living at the cabin ran to the saloon at the head of the park and organized a search party for the wounded man. They searched in all directions and followoing the trail from McCullom's cabin to the cabin of his brother John—about seventy-five yards away. Along the trail they found James McCullom's dead body and immediately sent a messenger for the authorities.

A constable started for the charcoal pits and found Gilbert, his partner, and Hendricks asleep on the charcoal dumps. The three men were arrested, but after the preliminary hearing, only Gilbert was held for trial. In May Gilbert was tried and convicted of the first-degree murder of McCullom and sentenced to hang on June 15 with another murderer, Merrick Rosengrants.

Merrick Rosengrants was born in New York in 1846. He was raised on a farm, but also found time to attend school and obtain a fair education.

While still a youngster he had a serious accident which left him crippled in one leg, causing him to limp noticeably. He was seized by gold fever when he was a young man and was one of the first to cross South Park, Colorado, and settle in the Ten Mile District of Colorado. In partnership with Colonel James McNasser, he built a sawmill at the head of Ten Mile Gulch near Carbonateville. He did quite a lively business until gold fever overtook him once again. He was convinced he could do better prospecting for gold than running the mill, and he sold his share of the business and began searching for a claim. Soon, though, he was as poor as any unsuccessful miner in the mountains.

Rosengrants's last prospect was to flume—a form of mining—in the Arkansas River, about six miles from Leadville. His claim adjoined that of John Langmeyer, and their camps were only a few hundred yards apart. In that desolate and lonely location, the two men naturally became close since no one else was around, but they were not friends.

On June 17, 1880, at about four o'clock in the afternoon, Langmeyer went to his camp to get an explosive cartridge to do some blasting. His tent was situated 150 yards above the ditch, on a steep and precipitous slope. As he approached the tent, he saw that the flap was turned back. He hurried through the opening to find a man crouched over his trunk, the lid open, and the burglar rifling through the contents. He immediately recognized the perpetrator as Rosengrants. Before he could speak, Rosengrants turned, pulled his five-shooter, and fired one shot. The ball missed its target, and Langmeyer turned and ran down the hill at top speed, with Rosengrants in as close pursuit as his crippled leg would allow. He fired four more shots, and one ball passed through the fleshy part of Langmeyer's thigh.

In his haste to escape, Langmeyer tripped over a log and fell very hard upon his stomach on a pile of rocks. He struggled to his feet and continued his downward flight, falling into the ditch, and crawling out the other side. He arose and staggered twenty more yards before falling again, this time unable to rise.

The sound of the shots alarmed a party of men burning charcoal three hundred yards away, and they ran toward the sound of the gunfire. They saw Langmeyer being pursued by a man with a peculiar, distinctive limp. The pursuer, when he saw the men coming, turned southwest and fled into the thick underbrush on the opposite side of the ditch, but not before passing before the men's view for several seconds. The rescuers arrived at the place where Langmeyer had collapsed, and he asked them to arrest Rosengrants for the attack. By then, however, the fugitive had escaped. A doctor was summoned and determined that Langmeyer had sustained serious internal injuries when he had fallen on the rocks. Inflammation quickly set in, and after sixty hours in agonizing pain, he died of infection. While Langmeyer languished on his deathbed, a close friend named John Gregory asked him if he could be mistaken in his identification of Rosengrants. The dying man replied, "No, John, that can't be possible, for I know him as well as I know you."

After Langmeyer died, a search began for Rosengrants, who was now conspicuously absent from his camp. When they could find no sign of him, they assumed he had fled east and would never be seen again, but eleven days later, Rosengrants appeared on Harrison Street in Leadville. He encountered a friend who, upon seeing him dirty and bedraggled, invited him to have a beer at the Carbonate Hall. As soon as the drinks were served, the friend excused himself and hurried to inform County Sheriff J. R. Tucker that the suspected murderer was in town. The sheriff hustled to the bar, arrested Rosengrants, and escorted him to jail.

Rosengrants was indicted for first-degree murder. During his trial in April, witnesses testified that Rosengrants was of the same height and build as the attacker, and he had the same peculiar limp they had noticed while watching the murderer flee. His conspicuous absence immediately after the murder didn't help his case, but the antemortem statement of Langmeyer was the most damaging evidence.

When the defendant took the stand, his defense was a long itinerary of where he had been during the murder and the following eleven days. However, even though he was well known in all parts of the country, he could not produce a single corroborating witness. The trial took six days and closed at 2:30 A.M.

The jury was out only a short time before returning a verdict of guilty as charged; they added the clause of felonious intent, which carried the death penalty. Motions for arrest of judgment and for a new trial were overruled by the judge. On May 25, 1881, Rosengrants was sentenced to hang on June 15—the same day as Francis Gilbert. The case was appealed to the Supreme Court, which advised the governor to grant a respite. The governor stayed the execution for forty-one days, until July 28, 1881. However, the appeal was expeditiously considered and denied, and no further interference was granted by the governor.

Rosengrants and Gilbert were imprisoned together in the Denver jail until the day of their execution. The condemned men slept well their last night and arose in good spirits at 5:00 A.M. They bathed, shaved, and dressed in their new burial suits. At 9:30 two carriages pulled up to the jail and the prisoners were brought out. Gilbert was accompanied by a priest, Sheriff Tucker, and a deputy; Rosengrants was accompanied by a priest, the undersheriff, and one deputy. When the carriages were filled, a signal was given for the captain of the cavalry to form the escort, and he placed two troopers at each carriage door. The procession moved through town and continued at a solemn pace to the gallows, two miles from the city.

The scaffold had been built using the counterpoise or "twitch-up" design, also sometimes called the New York or Brooklyn plan. These gallows were unique to the frontier West and consisted of individual weights for each man rather than the typical one-weight system. Specifically, this design used a 260-pound weight placed upon a table eleven feet above the platform. This great weight was dropped by turning

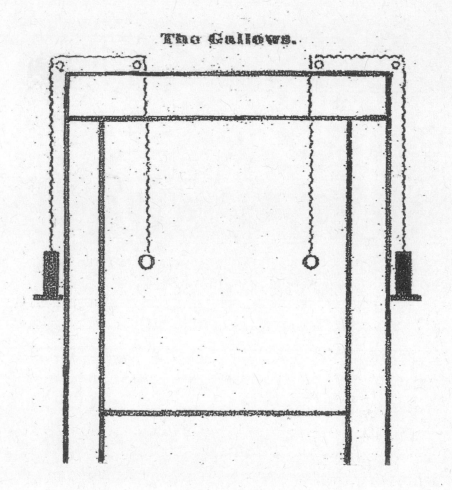

THE DOUBLE "TWITCH-UP" GALLOWS DESIGN

HANGING OF GILBERT AND ROSENGRANTS IN DENVER
ON A DOUBLE "TWITCH-UP" GALLOWS

the table, which was accomplished by releasing a small spring trigger. When the weight fell, the condemned men would be jerked upward. The gallows were surrounded by a rope barricade to hold back the crowd.

At 9:55 A.M. the gleam of bayonets appeared over the brow of the hill as the procession neared the scene, but at the slow pace it was traveling, it still took ten minutes to arrive. The procession was quite a spectacle. First came the militia unit of twenty-three men called the Sherley Guard, then Company F of the Carbonate Rifles, and close behind detachment of nine men from the Buena Vista Company.

The prisoners, priests, and guards made their way through the crowd—which numbered nearly ten thousand men, women, and children—and joined the thirty-five officials and reporters inside the roped barricade. As soon as the carriages arrived, Deputy Wesley Calvin took his position at the rear of the platform and prepared to activate the spring releases that would drop both weights. When everyone was in position on the low platform, a prayer was offered.

As soon as the priest concluded, the undersheriff stepped forward and read the death warrants and reports of the legal proceedings, first to Rosengrants and then to Gilbert. The undersheriff removed their handcuffs, and Rosengrants stepped to the front edge of the platform and made a lengthy speech to the crowd. Gilbert then stepped forward. Referring to the written statement he had prepared on June 13, he said only, "I have made all the statements I wish to the reporters. That is all." The priests then administered the last rites of the Apostolic Church to their parishioners.

When the religious ceremonies ended, a deputy commenced binding the men's limbs and the nooses were positioned. Sheriff Tucker pulled a black cap over Rosengrants's head while his undersheriff attended to Gilbert. At 10:30 A.M. Sheriff Tucker gave the signal by waving his handkerchief. Deputy Calvin activated the release, and the two men were simultaneously jerked seven feet off the platform and rebounded eight inches, breaking their necks. Gilbert appeared to die at once, but Rosengrants held on for thirteen minutes. An autopsy was held at 3:00 P.M., and the funeral for both men was held at 5:00 that evening.

The gallows on which Gilbert and Rosengrants were executed was one example of ingenuity in hanging men. In all about one fourth of the executions by hanging on the frontier were conducted on twitch-up gallows.

One Lynched
and Five Hanged
for the Bisbee Massacre

March 28, 1884

IT WAS JUST PAST 7:00 P.M. ON DECEMBER 8, 1883, when five men—"Big Dan" Dowd, Omer W. "Red" Sample, Daniel "Yorkie" Kelly, James "Tex" Howard, and William E. Delaney—rode into the small mining town of Bisbee, Arizona, in Cochise County. They tied their horses to a rail at one end of town and walked to the Goldwater & A. A. Castaneda store. Two men remained outside the store to watch the street, while the other three men entered.

Inside, the owner's wife and six patrons were completing their final transactions before the store closed. With guns drawn, the three robbers announced that this was a holdup. They forced Joseph Goldwater to hand over the money in the drawer, and then searched the living quarters of Jose Maria Castaneda, who was confined to his sickbed. Finding money and a watch under Castaneda's pillow, the robbers then turned their attention to the safe. They opened it, expecting to find the seven thousand dollar payroll for the Copper Queen Mine, but were disappointed when they learned it had not yet arrived by stagecoach.

Outside, J. C. Tappenier, assayer at the Copper Queen Mine, and D. T. Smith, a well-known rancher on the San Pedro River, were walking together toward the store. The two robbers who were posted outside each fired a single round from their Winchester repeating rifles. Both Tappenier and Smith were shot in the head and died instantly.

At the sound of gunfire, the town was aroused and several people began to run into the street, toward the scene of the shooting. As the town's citizens converged on the store, the two lookouts panicked and opened fire, shooting indiscriminately. J. A. Nolly was shot in the breast and lingered a few hours before expiring. Mrs. R. H. Roberts, a young pregnant woman, peered out of her door and was shot—the bullet passing entirely through her and severing her spine. She died a short time later.

The gang completed their robbery within a few minutes and hurried out of Bisbee with about three thousand dollars and two gold watches. Rewards of fifteen hundred dollars for each man, dead or alive, were soon posted and posses were formed. Deputy Sheriff William Daniels was put in charge of the investigation and the pursuit of the murderers.

Texas-born John Heith (sometimes spelled "Heath") was a dance hall owner and saloonkeeper at Bisbee. He and another man were hired as trackers, but when Heith only seemed to be leading the posse in circles, suspicion among the sheriff and his men began to ripen. Heith and the other tracker trailed the murderers as far as Soldier's Hole northeast of Bisbee, but then returned to Tombstone, where both trackers were arrested at gunpoint and lodged in Tombstone's jail for suspicion of being involved in the Bisbee Massacre.

Heith was believed to have planned the robbery or at least was involved in helping them get away. As soon as he was behind bars he began to "peach" on his fellow conspirators and named all five perpetrators of the "Bisbee massacre." Flyers were distributed announcing the men's names and descriptions, and the rewards for bringing them in. These circulars were also translated into Spanish and distributed below the border. At a preliminary examination, Heith was held to answer to the grand jury and subsequently jailed. The other tracker was released by the judge, when it was shown he could have had no part in the massacre.

After the robbery, the gang of five left Bisbee and proceeded east to Soldier's Hole, where they divided the booty and parted ways. Dowd and Delaney went south into Sonora, Mexico, while Howard, Kelly, and Sample turned north for Clifton, Arizona Territory.

About three days after the massacre, while passing through the Chiricahua Mountains in southeastern Arizona, Howard, Kelly, and Sample were discovered in camp near Galeyville. They were given chase by a posse led by a deputy U.S. marshal from Deming, New Mexico, who mistakenly thought the three men were part of the gang which derailed and robbed the train at Gage Station, New Mexico. However, the marshal was unable to catch the men, and all three Bisbee murderers were able to avoid the posse when a terrible snowstorm aided their escape.

The three fugitives continued north for a short distance when Kelly decided that the country was too warm. He left Howard and Sample at the railroad line and stole a ride on a freight train bound for Deming.

While traveling Kelly let his beard grow and allowed his general appearance to deteriorate for a time in hopes that he would pass as a tramp. At Deming, Kelly felt secure in his escape and went to the barbershop to clean up. Barber Augustin Salas, upon shaving his bushy client, immediately identified him as a wanted man and held a razor to his throat while a lawman was summoned.

Deputy Sheriff Daniels had tracked Kelly to Deming by following every credible lead, but lost all trace of him until summoned to the barbershop. At first Kelly was arrested on suspicion of being a train robber, but the Arizona deputy made his case to the local lawmen and was soon on his way to Tombstone with the first Bisbee murderer in irons. Kelly was turned over to Sheriff Jerome L. Ward on December 11, and charged in the deaths of four Bisbee citizens.

Sample and Howard continued on to Clifton in Arizona Territory. The *Clifton Clarion* reported that W. W. Bush was the night barkeeper at George Hill's saloon and was well acquainted with all of the Bisbee murderers. Bush was at Maud Elbi's brothel on Main Street when he was aroused from his slumber by the tramp of horses at the rear of the house and a tapping on the window. One of Maud's girls went to the window and asked, "Who's there?" The answer was "Red! Let me in." He said he desired to see Bush and the bartender at Hill's Saloon had informed him that Bush was at Maud's. Bush told the woman to open the door, and Sample and Howard entered. Sample went to the room where Bush had been sleeping, and after a salutation, Bush asked, "What are you doing here, and where have you been?" Sample replied, "Bisbee."

Bush asked him, "Do you know what you did in Bisbee, Red?" and Sample replied, "I think we must have killed someone! One man came running towards us; I told him to turn back; he replied, 'I am an officer,' and as he continued to advance, I shot him."

Bush then said, "Red, you boys are reported to have killed three men and one woman in Bisbee. If you had robbed the town without killing anyone, it would have been bad enough."

Sample informed Bush that he had taken eight hundred dollars and some watches, showing Bush a handsome gold watch. He said, "Johnnie Heith put up the job and opened a dance hall in Bisbee in preparation for the robbery." He also indicated that after leaving town, the gang kept together for a distance of nine miles before Delaney and Dowd decided to go to Sonora. Thirty miles north of Bisbee, a rancher had furnished them with fresh horses, and soon afterward Kelly took the train to Deming. Sample and Howard said they decided to go to Clifton and then on to Happy Jack's, about thirty-five miles away, where they would "get a crowd together to return and serve Clifton the same as Bisbee." Sample and Howard then headed off in the direction of Happy Jack's and Bush hurried to the Sheriff's office.

Deputy Sheriff John Hovey was awakened and Bush told of Sample's plans. Deputy Sheriff A. G. Hill was then summoned and a consultation was held. It was decided to temporarily await developments, as the numerical strength of the bandits was not known. Preparations were immediately begun in a systematic manner to pursue and capture Sample, Howard, and anyone else who planned to participate in the massacre at Clifton. Hovey and Hill were told that the reward of seven thousand five hundred dollars would be for the capture, dead or alive, of the whole number of Bisbee murderers; but for each individual offender, a proportionate amount was offered. The deputy sheriffs found Nicolas Olguin a local rancher who was ready to form a posse with a party of thirteen Mexican vaqueros in his employ.

By Friday morning, preparations were complete and the posse, numbering nineteen men—including Deputies Hovey, A. G. Hill, and Henry Hill; George Bent; W. W. Bush; and the Olguin party—headed north. Their progress was slow due to the pack animals they brought. By the end of the first day, they only made it as far as the confluence of the Blue and San Francisco Rivers. The following day they continued up the Blue, following a plain trail of three horses, which they were confident belonged to Sample and Howard. The posse grew as men from Benton's Ranch and Arnold's Ranch joined the group as they traveled along the Blue. The lawmen didn't want these men to aid the fugitives, so they were basically forced to go along with the group.

A short distance beyond Arnold's Ranch the posse halted and a lookout with field glasses was sent to the top of an adjacent mountain with instructions to view the surrounding country and report on the approach of any person. Only a brief period had elapsed when a signal was given that someone was approaching in the same direction the posse had recently come from. Quickly the men secreted themselves in the thick underbrush and awaited the intruder.

As the rider drew near, he was recognized as Howard. The fugitive was so utterly unaware of the trap set for him that he was within a

LYNCHING OF JOHN HEITH

few yards of the ambush before he discovered the muzzles of eighteen hostile rifles pointed at him. He heard the command, "Throw up your hands," and replied, "I don't propose to walk into anybody's graveyard!" Howard was taken prisoner.

Although the trail the posse was following led right on ahead, Howard had come upon them from the rear. The officers immediately realized that Howard had left the robbers' camp and gone around the mountains to make a fresh trail in an attempt to throw off the posse. They believed that Sample could not be far ahead. As night was approaching, it was decided to camp where they were and continue the search the following day.

The next morning the posse moved out of camp, and after continuing up the Blue for three miles, the trail suddenly turned into a narrow box canyon, or more precisely a crevice in the mountains not wide enough for two men to ride abreast. At the bottom of this canyon was a stream of water. The men decided to ascend the gorge afoot, and Nicholas Olguin stepped forward and proposed that he and his men would take on the task. The proposition was agreed to and soon Olguin and his party plunged into the cold waters, which rose nearly to the tops of their boots. They went up the canyon a distance of three miles to a point where the canyon widened out to a width of fifty yards. Just before it opened into a mesa, they came upon the robbers' camp.

In a moment rifles were leveled, and Sample was taken prisoner. He had been busy cleaning a revolver and two rifles when they came upon him, and not a single cartridge was in any weapon. Olguin searched him and found in his pockets two hundred dollars and a valuable gold watch with the name "Wm. Clancey" engraved on the inside of the lid and the monogrammed initials "W. C." on the outside. The watch fit the description of one taken at Bisbee. Olguin's men proceeded to break up the robbers' camp and return down the Blue. After joining the remainder of the posse, the march homeward began with Sample and Howard in custody.

Meanwhile Dowd and Delaney left their three companions for Sonora, Mexico. They traveled together as far south as Bavispe where Delaney left Dowd. He went to Magdalena, where he assumed the alias "Summers" and sought work. Unfortunately for Delaney, he had been recognized. Unaware, he continued on to the Total Wreck Mine in the town of Minas Prietas. The superintendent gave him a job, thereby detaining him until an American lawman arrived and his arrest secured.

Confident that Delaney would stay put, Deputy Sheriff Daniels decided to pursue Dowd first following him through perilous Indian country across the Sierra Madres and into Janos, Mexico. Arriving at Janos, he found that Dowd had just left for the mines at Corralitos. He went there, and with help from the superintendent of the mines in Corralitos, he arrested Dowd on New Year's Day. Dowd was driven to a station on the Mexican Central Railroad, locked in an express car, and brought onto American soil without the formalities of an extradition. Daniels then went after Delaney. He was arrested at Minas Prietas on January 15 and also returned to American soil without any formalities.

Now, finally, the five men responsible for the Bisbee Massacre plus Heith were captured and in custody. The six prisoners were indicted on February 8, and the trial commenced immediately. Three days later they were convicted of first-degree murder, and on February 19, the five Bisbee murderers were sentenced to hang. John Heith was only found guilty of second-degree murder, and on February 21, Judge D. H. Pinney sentenced him to life in prison.

The citizens of Bisbee and Tucson were outraged by Heith's sentence, as those serving life terms often served less time than those who had a set term, and pardons had been granted wholesale by governors over the previous decade. At an early hour the following day, a mob of one hundred men went to the courthouse and seven men went to the jail. Jailer Billy Ward thought it was the prisoners' breakfast being delivered, so he opened the door without checking and was taken prisoner.

TOMBSTONE TO DOCUMENT THE FIVE MEN WHO WERE
LEGALLY HANGED FOR THE BISBEE MASSACRE

The men opened Heith's cell and removed his shackles. They took him out to the waiting mob and drove their prisoner down Toughnut Street until they reached a telegraph pole. Heith requested that someone tie a handkerchief over his eyes and pleaded that they not shoot his body or mutilate it in any way after he was hung. His hands were tied, the noose was positioned, and he was pulled up to his death. Following the inquest, the coroner's jury reported, "We, the jury, find that John Heath [*sic*] came to his death from emphysema of the lungs, a disease very common at high altitudes. In this case the disease was superintended by strangulation, self-inflicted or otherwise."

On March 27, the day before the hanging of the five Bisbee murderers, the scaffold was tested and pronounced by experts to be one of the strongest and surest ever erected in the territory. The platform was eight feet from the ground, twenty-four feet long, and fourteen feet wide, with a five-foot drop, leaving three feet of clearance.

The doomed men slept well the night before their execution and arose that fatal morning in good spirits. They laughed and joked with those who were admitted to see them. The morning was occupied in shaving and dressing, then came the baptism of Howard and Sample and their confessions to their spiritual advisers. Nellie Cashman, a local sympathizer, was constantly with them during their last moments. Though talkative, they told her no secrets. The death warrant was read by Sheriff Ward at the request of the prisoners. Before leaving the jail, the five prisoners told reporters that they forgave all and hoped everybody would forgive them.

Precisely at 1:00 on March 28, 1884, the five condemned men walked freely to the scaffold, neither shackled nor handcuffed. When asked what they had to say, Sample spoke first. He asserted that he was an innocent man, that he wanted a Christian burial, and that Heith had been innocent. Howard and Dowd merely approved his remarks. Delaney added only that, although he was in the last stage of his life, if he had a fair trial, he would not have been hanged, implying his innocence as well. Kelly expressed a wish to have his religious advisor care for his remains. Of the five men, Delaney was the coolest. Dowd, who was very pale, said little, but while the rope was being put around his neck, he turned to the deputy saying, "Pull that tight." As the caps were put over their faces, all cried out, "Good-bye!" Their remarks occupied only three minutes and immediately afterward, at 1:18 P.M., the trap was sprung. All but Dowd, who convulsed for several minutes, died without a struggle.

The physicians declared all five men dead at 1:26 P.M. Two thousand people witnessed the execution; half of them were within the jail yard and the others sat on housetops in the vicinity. Immediately after the pronouncement of death, the crowd dispersed. By 2:00 P.M., the bodies had been cut down and conveyed to the morgue, where hundreds of curious citizens thronged to view the corpses. Upon examination, it was determined that all necks were broken except Dowd's, who had strangled to death. The following day the bodies were turned over to the Catholic Church for burial.

Bisbee remained a prosperous copper mining community until 1970, and then evolved into an artist's colony and tourist attraction. The town will always be best known, though, for the Bisbee Massacre.

Poor Andy!
From Slave to Grave

July 27, 1886

ANDREW "ANDY" GREEN WAS BORN into slavery near Lexington, Missouri, on June 15, 1862. Following the Civil War and emancipation, his family moved to Kansas City. Five years later he began his schooling, which continued for eight years. He learned quickly and was a mischievous youngster, often in trouble. As a youth, he stole from stores, friends, and neighbors—even from his own parents.

On September 27, 1874, Green stole a small bank from his neighbor William Dodd, broke it open, and found twenty dollars inside. He used five dollars to buy a .22 caliber pistol, which had only one cartridge. On September 29, Mr. Dodd questioned Andrew about the missing bank, and when Andrew denied any knowledge, Dodd went to Andrew's father. When his son continued to deny taking the bank, Pleasant Green gathered a rope and a knife and took his son into the woods. He declared that he was going to tie Andrew to a tree and whip him until he confessed, and then cut the rope to let him down. When they reached a tree that suited the purpose, Andrew came up behind his father, drew his pistol, and shot him in the back. He then hurried home and claimed that someone had shot his father.

Pleasant was brought home and the doctor was called, but the bullet could not be removed. However, the wound was not life threatening and Pleasant was soon able to receive visitors. Dodd then visited the Green household and requested permission to take Andrew with him for a wagon ride. As they traveled, Dodd said he was taking the boy to jail. A terrified Andrew finally confessed to taking the money and buying the pistol, and insisted that he had spent the remainder of the cash. The gun was returned to the gunsmith and the five dollars was recovered by Dodd. Dodd pressed Andy further and when threatened with jail again, he confessed to having shot his father. No punishment followed, beyond that meted out by Pleasant Green.

Andy quit school at the age of sixteen and took a job driving a delivery wagon for grocer H. F. Smith. Next, he worked in Robert McClintock's bakery situated near the Walnut Street theater. In order to gain admittance to the theater, he forged H. F. Smith's name for a supply of cigars from a local tobacconist, Beitman & Bros., which he used to bribe the doorman. On June 30, 1878, Andy was arrested for forgery and lodged in jail. He stayed there for six weeks before escaping on August 3.

To help him avoid a long prison sentence for forgery and escape, his parents gave him money to flee to Omaha, Nebraska, where he found work in a stationery store. He took to stealing again, but had limited success, so in the spring he took a job in a brickyard. That didn't last long, and he next moved back to Missouri, and then in 1880, he relocated to Wyoming. After some time working in the mines there, he started drinking and gambling.

It was in Wyoming that Andy befriended a miner named Allen Henderson. The two men, with six others, shared a cabin. One night in September, Henderson fought with a fellow miner, beat him badly, and took his money. A lynch mob of over three hundred miners came to the cabin looking for Henderson, but he was well hidden and they could not find him. When the crowd dispersed, Henderson and Andy fled to Medicine Bow, where Henderson was captured by the deputy sheriff.

ANDY GREEN'S VICTIM, JOSEPH C. WITNAH

Andy accompanied his friend to Carbon, where Henderson was tried and sentenced to three months in the county jail.

After Henderson was jailed, Andy went on to Denver, Colorado, and drifted into Leadville before returning to Missouri, where he took up work in the coalmines. Andy soon returned to a life of crime, and in May 1881, he was arrested for larceny and burglary. He was sentenced to five years in prison, but was released after three years and nine months. Following his release on April 22, 1885, he went home to Kansas City and swore to his mother that he would be an honest man from that point forward. He worked as a cook for three months, but when his health began to fail, he quit and returned to Denver.

In July 1885 Andy worked for Lewis & Scott for a brief time, but was soon stealing again. On October 21, 1885, he was sentenced to two hundred days in jail for stealing and after serving his sentence was released from custody on May 6, 1886. Less than two weeks later, Andy and his roommate John "Kansas" Withers concocted a plan to rob a streetcar.

Searching for an isolated place to wait for a car, Andy and Withers finally settled on a bench in front of Gallup's Garden just outside of town. They let three cars pass. When the fourth streetcar arrived and the two men saw that the street was empty of possible witnesses, they approached, Andy in front. He ordered the driver to hold up his hands, and then pulled his single-action six-shooter. It went off, and Andy, in the excitement, cocked it and fired a second time. The second ball killed the driver, Joseph C. Witnah. Withers ran at the first shot, and Andy took off immediately after firing the second. They took different routes back to town, and when Andy reached his home, Withers was already in bed asleep.

On May 23, after telling several close friends of the crime, Andy got drunk at Eva Catlin's bordello. He started a commotion and was arrested between Holladay and Blake Streets for disturbing the peace. He was put on the chain gang the following Monday because he couldn't pay the thirty-three-dollar fine, and was about to escape when he was charged with murder. Withers was also arrested and quickly confessed all the details of the murder. Feeling as if he had nothing to lose, Andy made a statement about the murder to the authorities on Tuesday evening, May 25, 1886.

The following day Andy had his preliminary hearing and was bound over for trial. Some time after midnight, he was aroused by loud noises and realized that the jail was under attack. A lynch mob of five hundred men, armed with picks and shovels and a few guns, fired at the jail and called out, "We want those murderers!" The large force of deputies, put on guard by the sheriff in anticipation of such an assault,

NEARLY 10,000 PEOPLE WATCHED ANDREW GREEN
EXPIATE HIS CRIME ON THE GALLOWS.

was up to the task. They returned fire and held off the mob. As more officers arrived, the leaderless mob dispersed.

The grand jury returned an indictment against Andrew Green and John Withers, and on June 16 they were asked to plead. Refusing to do so, a plea of not guilty was entered on their behalf and the trial was set for Tuesday, June 22. By 6:00 P.M. on Thursday, June 24, twenty-three witnesses had testified for the prosecution and the case was closed without a defense.

The following morning instructions were read to the jury at 10:00, and at 2:00 P.M. the attorneys began their closing arguments. The jury was out for one hour and twenty minutes before returning a verdict of guilty as charged. Edgar Cayless, Andy's attorney, filed a motion for a new trial, but it was denied. On July 3, Judge Victor A. Elliott sentenced Andy to hang on July 27, 1886, and sentenced Withers to life in prison.

As soon as Andy was returned to jail, he began to write an autobiography of fourteen brief chapters; he also composed several poems. During the week before his execution, a large number of men and women, under the direction of Reverend Elder Gray, attended to Andy's religious comforts. They prayed and sang hymns with him, and during the interludes Reverend Gray discussed the hereafter and the details of Andy's funeral.

The gallows had been erected at the bend of Cherry Creek, directly east of Smith's Chapel in West Denver. The design, known as a "twitch-up" gallows, operated by dropping a heavy weight tied to the end of the hangman's rope opposite the noose. The body of the condemned man was thus jerked upward.

On Andy's last night the choir from the Zion Baptist Church left after midnight, but there was little sleep to be had. A large crowd milled about the jail yard all night. In the morning Andy's attorney and reporters from Denver's *Rocky Mountain News* visited the prisoner. They were soon joined by Reverend Gray. At 10:00 the choir returned and they were closely followed by Reverend I. W. Tripplet of Denver's African Methodist Church. He was assisted by a reverend of the same church in Pueblo. The camp-style meeting ended after noon, and Andy dressed in his burial clothes: a black suit with a diagonal design, black necktie, white shirt, black socks, and black slippers.

The sheriff and his assistants appeared at the cell before 1:00 P.M. and escorted the prisoner to a hack awaiting them. With Andy were Reverend Gray, Attorney Cayless, and the sheriff. The procession was led by a large police force, and behind them was a hack containing a deputy sheriff, the county jailer, and visiting sheriffs. Next came the wagon of the undertaker, and bringing up the rear were several more

GREEN'S GALLOWS

hacks containing distinguished visitors, representatives of the press, and others invited to participate. Spectators were noticeably absent along the route, as thousands had already gathered around the gallows.

The procession arrived in a half hour, and at 1:40 P.M. Andrew Green stepped onto the platform. Police and citizens clutched hands inside the rope barricade to prevent the surging mass of twenty thousand people from crowding the gallows. Those who rode in Andy's hack stood at the edge of the platform, along with a choir. The lengthy death warrant was read by the sheriff and was followed by a hymn. Two of the five doctors in attendance came to the platform, shook hands with Andy, and then recorded his pulse at ninety-two beats, about twenty above normal. The crowd became excited at the appearance of the doctors, and a lieutenant from the Denver police force loudly announced, "The sheriff of this county commands you to stand back and not crush in these ropes."

Reverend Gray read scripture and several more hymns were sung. The condemned man then delivered a lengthy speech. When he concluded, his arms and legs were pinioned and the noose was adjusted. Andy yelled over the crowd noise, "Farewell, everybody!" as the black cap was pulled on by a deputy. At 2:20 P.M. the sheriff cut the restraining cord, the 310-pound weight dropped, and the prisoner was jerked up. Dr. W. W. Anderson and a second doctor from his team monitored Andy's pulse and pronounced his death at eleven and one-half minutes after the weight fell. There was reflexive muscle twitching for another eight minutes.

The body was cut down at 2:53 P.M. and examined by the team of five physicians, who determined that death was by strangulation. The body was then given in charge of the acting coroner, who immediately surrendered the remains to the undertakers. One of the undertakers put his hands inside the black cap and arranged Andy's tongue and closed his eyes before removing the cover. A funeral service was held on Wednesday, July 28, 1886, at Denver's Queen Rink. Andrew Green was buried soon afterward.

After Green's execution his autobiography was given to the *Rocky Mountain News* for publication. The work detailed the murderer's life from his earliest memories until just before he was escorted to the gallows. Green even illustrated his life story with sketches, which the newspaper had made into woodcuts for their July 27, 1886, edition.

Green was prolific during his final days and penned several poems. His farewell poem reads:

> My name 'tis Andrew Green, that name I'll never deny,
> I left my aged parents in sorrow for to cry;
> Little did they think that this should be my doom,
> To die upon the gallows, all in my youth and bloom.
>
> My parents nursed me tenderly, as you can plainly see,
> An always gave me good advice to shun bad company;
> To leave off night walking and shun bad company,
> Rise state prison or the gallows my doom would surely be.
>
> But bad company and liquors was all of my delight,
> All of my companions invited me out at night;
> Said if I commit a murder, hung I never shall be,
> Take warning boys, take warning, take warning from me.
>
> Me and my companion went out here not very far,
> I had to kill the driver in my object to rob the car;
> Then I drew the fatal pop and shot him to the heart,
> Leaving his dear little wife a protector from her to part.
>
> Afterwards I was compelled to run to make my escape,
> But Providence was above me; alas! It was too late!
> Now I am a prisoner, and this to be my doom –
> To die upon the gallows, all in my youth and bloom.
>
> The day of my execution the people will draw nigh,
> My father will come from the East to take his last view of me;
> He'll weep and fall into my arms and bitterly will cry:
> "Dear son, my darling boy, this day you are doomed to die."

First Woman
Hanged in Nevada

June 20, 1890

WHEN A MAN WENT MISSING IN CARLIN, Nevada, the explanation that he had sold out and gone East, seemed plausible. That is until his decaying, mutilated body was unearthed a year later. Now a husband and wife faced the gallows for first-degree murder. On Saturday, June 21, 1890, Elko's *Weekly Independent* newspaper described the scene:

> Elizabeth and Josiah Potts then sat down on chairs provided for them.
>
> "Have you anything to say?" was again asked.
>
> "We are innocent!" was the reply, repeated several times.
>
> Their shoes were then taken off and they were pinioned, she by James M. Dawley, ex-sheriff of Lander County, and he by Elko County Sheriff L. R. Barnard, assisted by several deputies from behind. During this process Josiah remained silent but Elizabeth uttered a few words directing how it was to be done.
>
> They were then told to rise, but just then Josiah said faintly, "Good-bye," and at the same time nudged Elizabeth with his pinioned hand.

They shook hands from their wrists and, leaning forward, kissed affectionately.

Only a week earlier, on June 13, the *Weekly Independent* had observed that "this will be the first legal execution of a woman on the Pacific Coast and it is a matter which will not reflect any credit on Elko County." (At this time Nevada was considered part of the Pacific Coast.) Only a select few would be permitted to witness the execution, and the editor, fearing that the large crowd would become unruly when they learned they could not see the hanging, warned, "Stay away from Elko on Friday, June 20, 1890."

Josiah Potts was born in Manchester, England, on October 12, 1842. He obtained a common school education and apprenticed as a machinist. Elizabeth Atherton was born in the same town on December 21, 1846. She met Josiah during her childhood, and romance blossomed during adolescence. They were married at St. John's Church in Manchester in December 1863. Two years later they emigrated to America and settled in Milwaukee, Wisconsin. Josiah found work as a machinist, while Elizabeth was a housewife and cared for their growing family. She would bear seven children over two decades. The last, her daughter, Edith, was born on July 4, 1883.

Eventually Josiah was hired by the Central Pacific Railroad, and the Potts family moved to Terrace, Utah, where the Central Pacific machine shop was located. In 1886 the Potts family moved again, this time to Nevada, where Josiah continued working for the railroad in their machine shop at Carlin. It was in Carlin that their troubles began.

Miles Faucett, a carpenter by trade, moved to Carlin in the spring of 1887, stating that he was prospecting for business opportunities. He lived with the Potts family for several months before purchasing a ranch seven miles from town, along with a wagon and a fine team of horses for transportation. Elizabeth continued to bake for

ELIZABETH POTTS, THE SECOND WOMAN
LEGALLY EXECUTED IN THE WEST.

Faucett and do his washing, which required him to visit her home several times a week.

On January 1, 1888, Faucett visited Ed Linebarger, a man he had befriended after moving to Carlin. He asked his friend to escort him to the Potts household, where he planned to demand repayment of a loan. (Likely Linebarger was asked to accompany him, so that he could serve as a witness to the transaction.) He told Linebarger that he knew Josiah had the money and also that he knew something of Elizabeth's background that she would not want generally known. If necessary, Faucett would threaten to expose her to compel repayment of the debt. However, when the men arrived, all was quite friendly. After spending some time in conversation, Elizabeth invited Faucett to remain the night as it had grown dark. Faucett agreed and Linebarger walked the short distance back to his home.

The next morning Faucett's wagon was still in Josiah and Elizabeth's yard, and his horses were in their stable. When Faucett was not seen for several days, foul play was suspected, and Sheriff Barnard was called to investigate. Josiah showed the sheriff a bill of sale for all of Faucett's property and explained that the missing man had suddenly been called to California on business. The signature on the receipt appeared authentic and everything seemed in order. With no evidence to the contrary, the matter rested.

During the summer of 1888, the Potts family—Josiah, Elizabeth, and their children—moved to Rock Springs, Wyoming, and George Brewer and his wife moved into the house they had vacated. On January 19, 1889, Brewer was remodeling the basement and in a corner, under a wooden shelf, he found the buried remains of a human male. The body was exhumed and found to have been horribly mutilated. A coroner's inquest determined that the remains were those of Miles Faucett, and the coroner's jury charged Josiah and Elizabeth Potts with his murder.

The couple was arrested in Wyoming and returned to the city of Elko for trial. In their defense they claimed that Faucett had, in August

JOSIAH POTTS

1887, tried to molest their youngest daughter Edith, who was but four years old at the time. Elizabeth discovered Faucett before he could abuse the child and prevented the crime. On the evening of January 1, 1888, Josiah first learned of the matter and threatened to report Faucett's offense. According to the couple, Faucett then signed over all his property to Josiah Potts, handed over his purse of gold coins, and fatally shot himself in front of the couple to prevent prosecution for such a contemptible offense.

Josiah said that he first laid Faucett's body on the bed and contemplated reporting the incident, but then, fearing he and Elizabeth might be charged with the murder, he buried the body in the basement. Several months later he took up the body, severed the head and feet, and tried to burn the remains. But the body would not burn, and the stench was so unbearable that he again buried the body and built a shelf over it.

Josiah and Elizabeth were placed on trial in Elko's district court beginning on Tuesday, March 12, 1889, with Judge Rensselaer R. Bigelow presiding. Son Charley Potts was sixteen years old when he testified about the evening Faucett disappeared. He said that he had gone to bed, but arose when he heard loud talking. He opened the door in time to see Faucett shoot himself, then went back to bed and said nothing to his mother. He did not know what had happened to the body as it was gone in the morning and was not curious to know. His parents never spoke of the incident except to tell him that if anyone asked, he was to say that Faucett had gone to California on business, which was precisely what he had told the sheriff when asked two years earlier. Charley said he knew he had not told the truth, but never asked his parents why they instructed him to lie. This caused one of the jurors, after deliberations, to observe that "his statement shows him to be quite shrewd for one of his age, but the most completely devoid of natural curiosity of any person we ever heard of."

Elizabeth's, Josiah's, and Charley's stories all agreed on every detail, and each family member held to it steadfastly. Josiah was a quiet, timid man of average size, while Elizabeth had a rather prepossessing appearance. Weighing more than two hundred pounds, she had piercing light blue eyes and a fresh complexion. According to the *Independent,* "Elizabeth's stoic demeanor throughout their trial suggested that she had been entirely in charge."

The evidence was concluded by Thursday, and the case was given to the jury on March 15 at 3:40 P.M. Their story, that Faucett had committed suicide to avoid being labeled a child molester, was so implausible to the jury they had presented their verdict in writing to the judge by 7:55 P.M. The jurors found that the pair "had cruelly, maliciously and premeditatedly took the life of an innocent and inoffensive old man for no other reason than to rob him of all he possessed and to avoid payment of a debt." The jury found both defendants guilty of murder in the first degree. Sentencing was scheduled for March 20, 1889.

In sentencing Josiah and Elizabeth, Judge Bigelow said:

> The mind naturally recoils with horror at the thought that anyone can become so lost to the common instincts of humanity, which teach us to rather relieve than add to the suffering of others, as to be guilty of the deliberate, premeditated and cruel murder of another. And yet experience teaches us that sometimes this is the case; but seldom indeed do we find that a woman has been the perpetrator. To her we look for everything that is gentle and kind and tender; and we can scarcely conceive her capable of committing the highest crime known to the law. But that such is the case here, it seems to me, there can be no reasonable doubt.

Elizabeth and Josiah were sentenced "to be hanged by the neck until you are dead." All appeals failed, and the application for commutation of sentence to life imprisonment was denied. The date for execution was set.

THE POTTS'S GALLOWS

The sun rose bright and clear on June 20, 1890. There were few people in the city of Elko for the occasion, except representatives of the press and several sheriffs and ex-sheriffs, who had been invited as witnesses. One of the reporters was from San Francisco's *Examiner.* During her interview with Elizabeth, she was told, "A woman would not kill a man to whom she was married." This careless comment piqued her interest and inspired her to investigate further upon her return to California.

The prisoners passed the previous evening quietly. Josiah slept throughout the night, but Elizabeth did not fall into deep sleep until about 3:00 A.M. When they awoke they had a light breakfast and seemed almost cheerful. At 7:00 they began to dress and make final preparations. As they busied themselves, Sheriff L. R. Barnard expressed concern for Elizabeth, but she assured him that she would "walk firmly to the scaffold and submit quietly to the inevitable."

Reverend M. Porter had been with the couple the previous evening and returned Friday morning to remain with them to the end. As he administered to their religious needs, they seemed composed, except that Elizabeth would sway in her chair each time feet shuffled outside the cell. At 10:30 A.M. ex-sheriff Dawley and Sheriff Barnard appeared at the cell door with a flask of whiskey. A drink was given to each of the condemned, and then Dawley read the death warrants.

Elizabeth raised her right hand and swore, "Innocent, so help me God!" and Josiah added, "We are innocent!" Another sip of whiskey was granted, and at 10:38 A.M. Josiah started out with Dawley, and Elizabeth with Barnard. The gallows was only a short distance from the door so they were able to make a calm, straight walk to the top in only a few moments.

At 10:40 they shook hands with the officers and minister and thanked them for their kindness. As the ropes were being adjusted, Josiah said, "Lord, have mercy on me," and Elizabeth echoed, "Lord have mercy on my soul." These same words were repeated several times as the black caps were drawn over their faces. At exactly 10:44 A.M. Sheriff Barnard cut the cord and the trapdoor dropped from beneath the feet of the two condemned prisoners.

Elizabeth's hands and feet quivered slightly and she died immediately, the carotid artery having been ruptured by the drop—as evidenced by a stream of blood. Only a few muscle twitches were noted in Josiah's body. The three attending physicians had to stand on chairs to monitor vital signs. They pronounced both of the prisoners dead at 10:53 A.M. Elizabeth's body was cut down at 11:07, and ten minutes later Josiah's body was also cut down. They were delivered to the undertaker with black caps still covering their faces. He hurriedly took them away to be prepared for the burial service at noon.

The small crowd of reporters and witnesses quickly dispersed at the sheriff's direction, but a few reassembled at the gravesite. At 12:10 P.M. the bodies were lowered into their graves, side by side. Twenty-five people, including half a dozen children, attended the funeral. Elizabeth and Josiah's children were not in attendance, as they were kept away by the families with whom they had been placed.

The reporter for the *Examiner*, Annie Laurie had an interview with Elizabeth which left important questions unanswered, and this just made her more determined to learn what Miles Faucett knew about Elizabeth—what secret of hers had Faucett threatened to expose in order to convince her to repay her debt?

In Sacramento, California, the reporter found the record of a marriage license issued on March 28, 1886, to "Miles Faucett, aged 56, a resident of Fresno, and Elizabeth Atherton, a widow, aged 38, a resident of England." They were married by a justice of the peace, and the ceremony was witnessed by Mrs. Lizzie Thomas, a marriage broker. It is unknown why Elizabeth left her family, went to California, saw a marriage broker, and became a bigamist.

The Faucetts lived together as man and wife, but Miles soon became suspicious of his new bride, who talked in her sleep and said things that suggested she was still married. Faucett made a few confidential inquiries and learned that Elizabeth had a husband living in Carlin, Nevada. The Faucetts soon separated, and a suit was filed against the marriage broker for recovery of the $105 fee paid for providing a wife. After the suit was settled, Elizabeth returned to her husband Josiah and family in Carlin. Faucett soon sold all his holdings in Fresno and also moved to Carlin, presumably to be near Elizabeth. Bigamy was a federal offense and could result in a lengthy prison term, so it was surmised by Laurie that Faucett's threat to report this crime might have been Elizabeth's motive for murder.

Regardless of the motivation, overwhelming circumstantial evidence proved that Elizabeth and Josiah Potts brutally murdered Miles Faucett. As a result, the Potts paid for their crime. Elizabeth Potts was the first woman hanged in Nevada, and the second in the entire West.

Enoch Davis
Dies by Firing Squad

September 14, 1894

THE ABILITY TO FACE DEATH BRAVELY WAS greatly admired on the western frontier. Back then a legal execution offered perhaps the sternest test of one's mettle, because death was certain and many spectators attended primarily to see how the prisoner comported himself. Few condemned men disappointed the crowd, but there were exceptions—and Enoch Davis was one. His behavior was so bad that Salt Lake City's *Daily Tribune* said, "[Enoch Davis] died like a dog, in fact, the most despicable mangy canine whelp that ever met an ignominious fate could not have whined itself out of existence in a more deplorable, decency-sickening state than was Enoch Davis' last hour."

A large colony of Mormons was established in Decatur County, Iowa, and the Davis family settled there for several years. Enoch was born there before the family continued on toward California. Enoch's father died on the plains, and his mother, with five small children, relocated to Wasatch County, Utah, in about 1860. Enoch and his brothers grew up and remained in Utah, and eventually Enoch married, but unlike other Mormons, he had only one wife. Despite the fact that he fathered nine children during the next twenty years, his marriage was marked by terrible quarrels, and his wife frequently threatened to leave. Enoch made counter threats to murder her if she followed through with her threats to leave, but they always reconciled.

In 1892 the Davis family, with eight of their children, was living in a one-room house in Ashley, a little hamlet in the northeast part of Utah. In late May of that year, Enoch and his wife had an argument that ended with the usual threats, but this time Mrs. Davis sensed something had changed and genuinely feared for her life. At 2:00 A.M. she fled the house and sought the protection of the sheriff. The next morning Enoch went to the sheriff's office, pleaded for forgiveness, and his wife again returned home.

On June 5 the couple quarreled yet again. Mrs. Davis wrote a letter to her sister, saying she was coming to live with her. She showed the letter to her husband, insisting that this time she was leaving him for good. Enoch flew into a terrible rage and made his usual threats, but in the end peace was restored and the family retired for the night. Mrs. Davis slept on the bed with the two youngest children, Enoch slept on the floor with the four next older, and the two oldest sons slept outside in the corral.

After his wife and children were all sleeping soundly, Enoch arose, took his heavy revolver off the wall, and crept to the bedside. He struck his sleeping wife with a heavy blow to the temple, carefully pulled her to the side of the bed, and then struck her a second time. The blows proved fatal, and Enoch waited until the blood stopped flowing before carrying her body to the vegetable garden and burying her in a potato hole. He returned to the house, cleaned up the blood, and then lay down to sleep. Everything had been accomplished with such stealth that none of the children awoke.

In the morning Enoch told his children that their mother had flown into a rage during the night and left for her sister's home. Toward evening, however, he could no longer contain the horrible secret. He told the second oldest boy that during the night his mother had committed suicide, and that she had asked him to bury her in a field three miles from the house. He warned his son not to say anything to anyone and said, "She died like a lady and I buried her like a gentleman." However, the boy had seen too many quarrels between his parents and heard too many threats. He feared that his mother had met with foul play, and he wasted no time leaving the family home to inform an officer that she was missing under suspicious circumstances.

As soon as Davis realized his son had left, he mounted his horse and fled into the Uintah Reservation. He was captured there three days later and was returned to Ashley. A search for Mrs. Davis was organized, and her body was soon discovered beneath the ooze and slime of the potato hole.

The citizens of Ashley were outraged, especially the women. It was only through the greatest efforts of the officers that they were able to prevent Enoch's lynching. The following day the prisoner was moved to Provo, and in October he was put on trial. The principal witnesses against him were his own children. The evidence, though circumstantial, was quite convincing. Enoch's defense was that he had found his wife in a compromising situation with a certain Dr. Butler and accidentally killed her. However, two credible witnesses proved that Dr. Butler was some distance away at the time of the murder.

The jury found Enoch guilty of first-degree murder without a recommendation for mercy. Motions for a new trial and an arrest of judgment were overruled, and on November 3, 1892, Judge John W. Blackburn sentenced Enoch to die by firing squad. When the judge concluded, "And may God have mercy on your soul; ask Him for His forgiveness and perhaps it may be granted you," Enoch surprised everyone by responding with sarcasm, "Well, I guess there's no copper on that," meaning forgiveness had no value for him.

He was taken to the state prison in Salt Lake City to await his execution. The case was appealed to the territorial court and then to the U.S. Supreme Court, but the judgment of the lower court was affirmed

WOODCUT OF ENOCH DAVIS

each time. Enoch was sentenced to death three times: first on November 3, 1892, for execution on December 30, 1892; second on April 10, 1893, for execution on June 9 of that year; and third on July 31, 1894, for execution on September 14, 1894. The prisoner's final hope was a petition to Governor Caleb W. West, pleading for commutation of the sentence to life imprisonment, or at least a respite. On Friday morning, Deputy U.S. Marshal Nat M. Brigham told the prisoner, "Well, Davis, it has gone against you. The Governor says the law must take its course."

The marshal asked what he wanted during his last hours and Enoch requested "good whiskey," which was supplied in ample quantities. Supposedly to confess, he asked to see defense attorney M. M. Warner, Esq. and Eugene Traughber, a reporter from *The Salt Lake City Tribune*. Enoch had been housed in a second-floor cell for months, but on Thursday he was moved to a corner cell on the ground floor in preparation for the trip to the place of execution. Warner and Traughber arrived at the penitentiary at 3:00 P.M. and were shown into the prisoner's new quarters by Warden Felix J. Stark. Enoch complained about his treatment by the governor, and no amount of prompting could get him to confess. He reported that he had slept well every night from midnight until 5:00 or 6:00 A.M., and he said he expected to sleep well his last night. He had maintained a hearty appetite throughout his incarceration. When asked if any clergy had been to see him, he responded with a stream of profanities, concluding, "God damn 'em, I don't want them to come, either!"

Sheriff Thomas Fowler was certain that a large crowd would complicate an execution by firing party. He was determined to limit the number of spectators, so he staged a ruse. With the help of a deputy, the two men pitched a tent to make the curious believe that the execution was going to take place in the jail yard.

The deputy then secured a common covered road wagon and loaded a large square tent, some bedding, a number of planks, a common congress chair (a wooden chair with arms), a plain board coffin, some carpenter's tools, and six .38–90 caliber Winchester rifles. Six "crack-shots" of steady nerve, chosen from a field of many applicants, climbed aboard. Each man had with him a long black alpaca shroud fitted to cover him from head to foot and protect his anonymity. The party drove to the site chosen at Dry Hollow and unloaded the materials.

Enoch spent his last night in his cell under a close guard, to prevent suicide, constantly attended by Dr. John S. Witcher. He was restless and called for whiskey, which was supplied. He awoke for a moment at 2:00 A.M., then slept again, and arose at 6:00. He ate a light breakfast and then started the long wagon ride from the Salt Lake City prison to his death. He seemed cheerful from the liquor and began telling vile stories filled with graphic detail and profanities.

The place selected for the execution was an isolated spot about two miles beyond the county line, commonly called Dry Hollow. The tent had been pitched at the bottom of the wash, and the scenery was a dreary one. There was little but sagebrush for miles around—except that right on the spot chosen for the execution were several patches of native mountain oak. The tent was pitched behind the tall plants so that it would not be seen from the road or from the railroad tracks two miles distant. Inside were planks on which the executioners would rest the muzzles of their guns. During the morning hours the deputy sheriff stepped off thirty paces and positioned the chair, which was made fast with stakes in the ground. On the back of the chair, wooden planks were lashed to stop the bullets.

Following breakfast the six executioners practiced firing unloaded weapons simultaneously, with the deputy marshal commanding, "Make ready. Aim. Fire!" Even though they were firing empty weapons, the deputy sheriff courageously took the convict's seat to be their practice target, staring into the muzzles of the rifles.

After the practice session, the executioners lay in the sun for a while. When a newspaper reporter arrived unannounced, he was kept away while the men scurried into the tent and donned their shrouds. A little before 10:00 the deputy marshal rode out to watch for the wagons. Twelve minutes later the first wagon from Salt Lake City arrived with several members of the press on board. The reporters were allowed to examine the place of execution. A crowd of two hundred curious spectators also arrived from Provo, those few who had learned of the ruse at the jail yard. They took up positions on the high ground some distance away. Among those who arrived at the site were James Davis, Enoch's brother, and two of Enoch's sons, seventeen-year-old Berlden and fourteen-year-old Archie.

At 10:40 A.M. the prison procession came within sight. In the first wagon was Deputy Marshal John L. Weber of Park City and W. C. A. Smoot, a prison guard. They brought with them the coffin, drugs, and food. Next came the wagon of the condemned man. Enoch wore manacles and was closely watched by Dr. Witcher, Warden Stark, Deputy Andrew Burt, and a prison guard named Marion D. Hoge. Bringing up the rear was Marshal Brigham's party, consisting of Chief of Police Arthur Pratt, Police Captain John N. Donovan, Deputy Marshal Edward W. Exum of Ogden, and witness J. P. Bache. Guards were sent out to the north and south to keep the crowd from advancing on the wagons and the place of execution.

Enoch wore a neat black suit with white collar, black tie, and a dilapidated white hat. Upon his arrival he greeted everyone with "Good morning, boys." He was under the influence of the liquor he had been drinking freely during the trip, which made Berlden Davis angry. Berlden complained that it was "a damned shame that my father should be allowed to get so intoxicated that I could not talk intelligently with him." Everyone dismounted but Enoch, who remarked, "I haven't got any nerve." At that point his defense attorney, M. M. Warner, stepped up and told him to brace up, and that his sons wanted "that the old man would die game." Enoch seemed worried that he wouldn't have a chance to talk to the people, but was assured that he

SCENE OF ENOCH DAVIS'S EXECUTION

would. Nonetheless, he shouted profanities and called loudly for pros-
titutes to step forward, an attempt to offend and embarrass those who
had come to watch him die. His behavior was so bad that the *Tribune*
reported:

> He could not utter five words during his last hour on earth
> that were not coupled with obscenity, blasphemy, vulgarity, and
> profanity. . . . His own cowardly tears fell through the foulest of
> breaths during his last hour, his complete lack of nerve, which
> under the circumstances might have won him a little human
> sympathy if it were not for his vile and lying tongue, reiterating
> the lie that his wife's death was an accident and claiming his own
> execution to be murder. Finally, with death only a few minutes

off, he repeated again and again, in his whining, maudlin way, always and ever hoping to the last that a reprieve would arrive at any moment to save him, that he was innocent, even denying his own confession at the trial.

Because the last half of the nineteenth century on the western frontier was a time when men were admired for facing death bravely and dying game when necessary, Enoch Davis's behavior was regarded as an embarrassment to everyone present, especially his brother and sons.

At 11:25 A.M. Marshal Brigham read the death warrant, which had been signed by Judge H. W. Smith. Enoch asked for something to eat and a large cup of coffee, but no coffee was present. He was given a sandwich and then he asked for more whiskey, which was provided. He was asked to make a confession for the newsmen, which resulted in a particularly vile string of profanities after which he was taken from the buggy and escorted to the chair by Andy Burt and Dr. Witcher, surrounded by penitentiary guards and lawmen. When placed in the chair, Enoch remarked, "Say, boss, this is no fair shake. This is altogether too close to them guns." He was told to be quiet.

Next Enoch complained that he did not want his hands bound. Marshal Brigham asked, "You will sit like a man, will you?" Enoch replied, "I'll set, you bet I will, but take them things off," indicating the cuffs. The cuffs were removed, but it was quickly realized that Davis was too drunk to sit straight, so small straps were brought over. When the condemned man saw them, he began to yell, "No, you don't put them on me." He tried to fight off the guards, but he was strapped to the chair in a sort of harness that bound his torso to the plank on the back of the chair and his hands to the chair arms. Dr. Witcher stepped forward and pinned over his heart a prescription blank with a black mark the size of a silver dollar in the center. The doctor then blindfolded the condemned man. As he did this, he bent over and whispered something to Enoch that caused him to nod his head.

Marshal Brigham ordered everyone to move away while the deputy marshal moved to the tent and gave the commands. At "Make ready," six rifle muzzles poked through portholes; at "Aim," the guns steadied; and at "Fire," all six weapons discharged as one. Enoch's body gave a sudden twitch and sank limp and lifeless. Dr. Witcher and Dr. Samuel H. Allen of Provo, with Traughber from the *Tribune*, rushed to the chair. The doctors felt for a pulse while the reporter recorded their conversation. At 11:44 A.M. all signs of life were gone and Enoch Davis was pronounced dead. Four balls had struck the prescription blank. Enoch's face presented a ghastly appearance, and Marshal Brigham covered it with a new black silk handkerchief. Soon the body was removed from the chair and placed in the coffin brought along for the purpose. The entire party started back to the penitentiary and arrived late in the afternoon. At that time Enoch's body was given over to the charge of the prison warden. No autopsy was performed.

Enoch's body was placed in one of the prison apartments, rooms maintained for visiting dignitaries but usually vacant, until the following day—Saturday, September 15, 1894. On Sunday the body was taken to the prison church, where the prisoners were allowed to pass in squads and view Enoch's remains. He was then buried in a grave outside the prison walls until relatives could call for it. It is undocumented whether family ever came, but it is certain that Enoch paid for murdering his wife.

Wife Murderer Charles H. Thiede Hanged

August 7, 1896

SALOON OWNER CHARLES H. THIEDE had physically abused his wife, Mary Frank Thiede, for years. On April 30, 1894, he murdered her with a knife so brutally that he nearly beheaded her. In a state where most condemned men chose death by shooting, Thiede opted for the gallows. The state selected the "twitch-up" design, and on August 7, 1896, the wife murderer was jerked to his death

Charles H. Thiede had been living in Utah since 1886 where he owned several ill-reputed saloons. Charles lived with his wife Mary in a house a short distance from his West Side Saloon. For years there was scarcely a time when Mrs. Thiede did not bear the traces of brutal beatings suffered at the hands of her husband. This was especially true when her husband was intoxicated, which was all too often.

After 7:00 P.M. on the evening of April 30, 1894, the Thiedes had supper with Charles's sisters and their husbands. Afterward the entire party went to the West Side Saloon to drink beer. A little after 9:00 a certain Mrs. Blohm and Miss Lillie Birch came in for wine and they joined the Thiede's party to visit. According to Charles, after all the visitors left, he sat on a couch in the bar and read the newspaper to his wife. He said that when he finished reading, she also departed for home, leaving him to tend bar. Charles claimed that at about 12:30 A.M., he stepped out of the saloon, saw a light at his house, and went to investigate. He said that the door was locked and he had to crawl in through a window, but once inside he found nothing unusual—except that his wife was absent. As he returned to the saloon, he discovered his wife's body, face down in a pool of blood, some fifteen feet east of the saloon.

Charles ran to Jacob Lauenberger's house to get help, and Dr. Wiley E. Ferrebee was summoned. Mary's body was carried into the saloon by the doctor and Lauenberger; Charles carrying a lantern to light the way. Her body was placed on a pool table to facilitate the doctor's examination. Charles at first told them that he thought she had committed suicide, but Lauenberger said, "That can't be, for there is no knife here." Charles then proposed that someone had tried to rape, or "outrage" her as the papers reported, but there was no evidence of such an attack.

The doctor found that Mary's throat had been cut so deeply that the jugular veins were severed as well as her windpipe. He determined that it had taken at least two slashes to inflict the wounds and these had nearly beheaded the woman. It also appeared that she had fought for her life; one of her fingers was nearly severed and it was speculated that she had thrown up her hands to ward off the knife. The doctor also noted that her house key was in her pocket.

At 4:00 A.M. Sheriff William McQueen was notified of the murder. With Deputy John Montgomery Jr. he went to the saloon to investigate. When they arrived, they saw Charles Thiede at the south door, but he immediately retreated to the bar and poured himself a drink. When they approached him, the sheriff asked, "What's the matter here?" Charles answered, "I killed my wife last night." When the sheriff told him he was under arrest, Charles changed his story and denied the killing, saying men of the Industrial Army were the murderers. After a short scuffle Charles was tied down to prevent his escape.

From the nature of Mary's wounds, the sheriff concluded that the murderer would have to be covered in blood—as blood had splattered as far as the outside wall of the saloon, more than fifteen feet from the place of the attack. Charles was covered with blood, which reportedly could not have happened after Mary's heart had stopped beating, but Charles first claimed that she was dead when he found her. This established the first discrepancy in his alibi. He would later change his story to explain being soaked with blood saying that she was alive when he found her, that he had lifted her into his arms, and that she had said, "Oh! Charlie!" as she died. However, this alternative explanation was no more plausible since she could not have spoken with the injury to her windpipe. This claim would eventually go against him at trial.

The sheriff next made a search for the murder weapon. He believed it to be a large bread knife that he had previously seen behind the bar on a recent visit to the saloon. The knife was missing and Charles would give no clue as to its whereabouts. The weapon was never found.

During the investigation nearly fifty men from the Industrial Army barracks gathered at the saloon. When they learned of Charles's accusation that some of them were the murderers, they called for him to be immediately hanged. To prevent a lynching, Deputy Montgomery ushered his prisoner into a buggy and hurried him off to Harry Haynes's store in Murray. From there he was transported to the county jail in Salt Lake City.

Charles was indicted by the grand jury and tried before Judge George W. Bartch in October. He was convicted of first-degree murder and sentenced to hang on November 5, 1894. The case was appealed to the Supreme Court, which affirmed the lower court's decision on June 13, 1896. Judge Ogden Hiles sentenced Charles to hang on Friday, August 7, 1896. Charles's last hope was a petition to Governor Heber M. Wells, but this was denied.

CHARLES THIEDE AS HE APPEARED IN HIS CELL SHORTLY
BEFORE HIS EXECUTION.

Charles Thiede continued to proclaim his innocence to the end. He proposed that the entire matter—the killing of his wife and his conviction for the murder—had been a scheme to cheat him out of substantial property holdings. Deputy Montgomery investigated this latest claim and found out that every bit of Charles's property was heavily encumbered; he was so deep in debt that several creditors went unpaid when the property was sold, and even his defense attorney had to accept a reduced fee. Montgomery was then accused by Charles of being part of a conspiracy to deprive Annie, his eleven-year-old daughter, of her inheritance.

Charles never gave up hope on receiving a reprieve, but by Monday, August 3, 1896, his family realized that all arguments and petitions had failed. They visited freely throughout Thursday, his final day, when they bade him a last farewell. During this last parting with his daughter, he nearly broke down. The prisoner sent word to Sheriff Harvey Hardy: "Tell the Sheriff that I will be in heaven a long time before he comes, and when he does I will meet him and show him around."

On his last night he was attended by Reverend L. B. Coates of the Church of Christian Science, along with a large number of his parishioners, and by Reverend James D. Gillian of the Liberty Park Methodist Church. After his visitors left Charles talked with his deathwatch guards until he retired at 2:00 A.M. The condemned man slept soundly until awakened by his guards after 6:00 A.M. He had been shaved by a deputy sheriff the day before, as they would not allow him to have a razor, so he had only to make his toilet and dress in his burial clothes—a black broadcloth suit, white shirt, dark tie, slightly worn Prince Albert hat, and slippers.

He was unable to eat solid food, but he drank a cup of coffee and an hour later had a glass of milk. At 8:30 A.M. Mrs. Louise C. Koenan of the Church of Christian Science arrived, and an hour later they were joined again by the two clergymen. Doctors E. S. Wright and

Albert Bower arrived at 9:00 A.M. to administer such stimulants or drugs as the condemned man might need, but Charles insisted he could withstand the ordeal and would not see them. Nevertheless, Dr. Wright was allowed to see the prisoner shortly before the procession began; he found Charles composed and cheerful.

Sightseers had begun arriving outside the jail as early as 5:00 A.M., and the crowd swelled to hundreds as the time approached. They expected the prisoner to be conducted through the jail yard to the scaffold, affording them a view of the condemned man minutes before he hanged. However, the route through the building to the scaffold chosen by Sheriff Hardy was entirely through inside passages, and Charles exited the jail building within the tall board enclosure surrounding the gallows.

The enclosure had been built behind the jail and measured seventeen by thirty-five feet. On two sides were upright boards eighteen feet tall, the jail wall comprised the third wall, and the fourth wall was a canvas screen that cut off the view from the north. The scaffold, built of Oregon fir by the firm of Willard & Stewart at a cost of $150, was fourteen feet high and painted black. The hanging rope passed through a hole in the crossbeam, over two pulleys, and down the side, where a 430-pound weight was attached. Under the noose was a low wooden platform upon which the condemned man was to stand while being prepared. In the entire construction of the gallows, not a nail or pin was used; it was bolted together so that it could be disassembled and used again. The one-inch rope was of silk hemp and had been tested several times on Thursday using a sack of gravel weighing 240 pounds to simulate the prisoner's weight; the apparatus jerked the sack three feet into the air.

The man who would set the machinery in motion was concealed behind a canvas screen. Upon the signal being given, he was to pull a lever to drop the weight.

It was nearly 10:00 A.M. when Sheriff Hardy ascended the winding staircase to Charles's cell on the second floor and read the death warrant to the prisoner. When he concluded the reading, Charles cried as he thanked the sheriff and his assistants for their treatment while he was in jail, and then he prayed and offered a blessing for the sheriff. All these proceedings took a half hour, and just before 10:30 A.M. the procession formed and marched down to the basement. There they halted while the heavy straps were applied to Charles's arms, but at his request his left hand was left untied. County Attorney Whittemore was on the telephone with the governor to ask, at Charles's insistence, if there was any chance of a stay, but the governor said there was not. When told of the remark, Charles visibly braced up once more.

At 10:35 the procession was again formed, and the march began up the flight of stairs and into the enclosure. The sheriff led the way with the Methodist reverend and a jail guard following, and close behind them was the reverend of the Christian Science Church leading the prisoner. The condemned man had a deputy at each arm for support.

At the platform the procession parted and the prisoner walked through the witnesses to take his place beneath the noose. As the prisoner gazed about, the sheriff asked, "Charles Thiede, have you anything to say before being hanged?" Charles answered, "I have been convicted of murdering my wife. I did not do it. For the last time on earth I announce my innocence of the crime." As he spoke he reached into his coat pocket with his free left hand and pulled out a sealed envelope addressed: "To be published after my death, Charles H. Thiede." He handed it to Whittemore.

Immediately after the prisoner concluded his speech, four deputies, working in two-man teams, completed the preparations for the hanging by binding his left hand and legs with the heavy straps. His wide-brimmed black hat was removed, a black cap was pulled over his head, and the noose was adjusted. At 10:39 the sheriff pulled his handkerchief from his pocket and waved the signal. The lever was thrown, the weight dropped, and the prisoner was jerked into the air.

At first there were short intervals of muscular contractions, followed by convulsive tremors, but soon the body hung motionless. Drs. Wright and Bowers checked Thiede's pulse and found it had decreased from one hundred twenty to fifty-four; it finally ceased at 10:54 A.M. Life was pronounced extinct, the black cap was removed, and it was determined that death had resulted from strangulation. The body was left hanging as Whittemore opened the letter and read the contents to the witnesses, wherein Charles Thiede had merely repeated his claim of innocence.

A steel cot was brought forward and placed beneath the body, and the remains of the prisoner were lowered onto it. The body was given over to the charge of the undertaker, Joseph William Taylor, who was representing the family. He placed Charles's body in a coffin and drove to his funeral parlor on West Temple Street. A brief funeral service was delivered by each of the reverends at 12:30 P.M. and by 1:00 Charles's remains were on their way to Sandy, Utah, for burial. Mrs. Thiede had been buried in Murray, but as one of Charles Thiede's final requests, she would later be exhumed and interred next to her husband in Sandy.

Parker Punished for the Jailbreak Murder

June 10, 1898

WHEN FLEMING "JIM" PARKER ATTEMPTED a train robbery in 1897, he soon found himself behind bars in Prescott, Arizona Territory. From there matters only went from bad to worse. During a jailbreak he murdered the county attorney and was sentenced to hang for the brutal shotgun killing. On June 10, 1898, Parker was "dropped into eternity" on the courthouse plaza at Prescott.

Parker and Jim "Harry" Williams (alias Charles or John Creighton, sometimes spelled Crayton) were cowboys working for the Arizona Cattle Company near Flagstaff and living in a cabin owned by the company. Parker was a horse breaker, and was exceptionally good at his trade, finishing well in Prescott's 1895 bronco-busting tournament. Williams was a cowboy who claimed to have been in Buffalo Bill's Wild West Show. They enjoyed the thrilling life of the cowboy, but there was never enough excitement or money to finance their wild sprees so they decided to try what others had done to enhance their fortunes—they decided to rob a train.

In December 1896 they burglarized two nearby cabins and took two Winchester rifles, food, and several "Selsor" shirts, which they cut up for masks. Parker and Williams enlisted the help of cowboys Abe

Thompson and Lovell "Love" Martin. Parker told Martin that they were going to rob a train, but they did not want Martin or Thompson to take part, except to help them with the get away. Parker sent Martin and Thompson into Peach Springs for ammunition and dynamite. Martin bought .40-60 ammunition at Watkins' Drug Store and .44 and .45 ammunition at Taggart's General Store in Kingman. Thompson bought two sticks of dynamite at Mickey Nelson's barn in Peach Springs. Parker and Williams each had one of the stolen Winchester rifles, and in addition Martin and Thompson gave up their six-shooters to the two aspiring train robbers.

On the day before the robbery, Martin obtained two fresh horses. He and Thompson went into Peach Springs, where they made themselves conspicuous to establish an alibi. According to the plan, they would be robbed of their fresh horses while returning to their cabin. Parker and Williams would then flee north on the two fresh horses, cross the Colorado River into Nevada, and camp at a spring familiar to all four men. Martin and Thompson were to return to town, turn loose the spent horses they had traded with the train robbers, report the theft of their fresh horses, and then misdirect the posse which was sure to follow in pursuit. After ten days, Martin and Thompson were to meet Parker and Williams at the camp in Nevada.

On the bone-chilling evening of February 8, 1897, Parker and Williams, carefully masked in black, hid eight miles east of Peach Springs, near milepost 457. At 7:15 P.M. they captured night watchman Edward Allen. Twice, freight trains came through, but finally at 8:50 P.M. passenger train No. 1 appeared, and Parker forced the watchman to flag the train.

The engineer signaled with two blasts of his whistle to acknowledge Allen's sign for danger and stopped the train. Engineer Bill Daze asked Allen to explain the problem ahead, but he received no answer. At that moment a masked man entered the cab of Engine 85 and took charge at gunpoint.

The two robbers took the fireman, engineer, and watchman to the rear of the express car, where they instructed the fireman to uncouple the remainder of the train. Parker then took the men back to the engine, while Williams remained on the rear platform of the express car. His job was to guard against interference from anyone in the passenger cars. He fired five shots along the side of the train to keep the passengers inside. Parker, once back in the engine cab, ordered Daze to pull the engine forward two miles to Nelson's Siding and then fired one shot into the air, a signal to Williams that he was still in control of the engine.

While the express cars were being uncoupled from the passenger cars, an express messenger, who was alerted by the unscheduled stop and several gunshots, armed himself with a .45 caliber revolver. With the help of a second express messenger, he jumped from the opposite side of the express car. Together they ran toward the rear of the train. When they reached the rear platform, they came face-to-face with Williams, who was armed with a Winchester rifle, a revolver, and two sticks of dynamite.

The armed messenger did not hesitate, and fired two shots in rapid succession. The first ball took effect in Williams's breast, just above his heart, and passed entirely through his body. As the robber slumped to the ground, the second ball struck him in the left eye and exited at the back of his head, killing him instantly.

The engine, tender, express car, and mail car pulled ahead to Nelson's Siding and stopped. Parker took Allen, the watchman, with him and found the express unguarded. Parker then went into the mail car, where he waved mail clerk A. S. Grant aside at gunpoint and went through the registered mail. He selected nine packages that looked as if they contained valuables, and then ordered Daze to back the engine up about halfway toward the passenger cars. Parker fired four shots into the air, apparently as some sort of a signal to Williams, and looked north of the tracks as if expecting someone. There was no reply to his signal, so the engineer was ordered to drive the engine back to Nelson's Siding. Once there, Parker said, "Get out of here as soon as God will let you," and then walked off into the brush.

Daze backed his engine to the passenger cars, coupled them to the mail car, and continued on to the next destination, where the robbery was reported. The most substantial clue was Williams, the dead bandit on the rear platform of the mail car. He was described as 147 pounds and 40 years old and was soon identified as a former employee of the Arizona Cattle Company. It was thought that the other robber was probably an acquaintance of his from the same place.

Back in Peach Springs, Thompson and Martin made certain that they were seen throughout the day in the event they needed an alibi. After sunset Thompson went to bed and Martin wrapped his feet in saddle blankets and went up on the hill to watch for the two robbers to come into view, his signal to wake Thompson and deliver the horses. When neither of the robbers appeared, Martin went back into town and prepared to go to bed. When he arrived, he found that Thompson was awake and had been about the town gathering intelligence to find out what happened to Parker and Williams.

Thompson reported that Parker and Williams had made a failure of it and Williams had been killed. They returned to Thompson's cabin to wait for Parker, but it was not long before they were arrested. Despite their best attempts to avoid any connection to the train robbery, it was well known by many that the four men were closely associated. Martin quickly weakened and confessed, and on March 22 he wrote and signed his confession. He turned state's evidence against Parker and Thompson and was released; Thompson remained behind bars.

Sheriff George C. Ruffner of Yavapai County, with deputies Martin Buglin, Ed Riley, and Tom Rogers were soon on Parker's trail. Indian trackers—probably Yavapai or Navajo—were employed to assist. The pursuit was mostly on foot, as Parker had intentionally chosen the most rugged terrain in that part of the country for his escape. On Sunday afternoon Ruffner, Buglin, and Riley fell back on their trail to butcher a beef to feed the posse, while Rogers went ahead with the Indians. Rogers and the others soon stumbled upon Parker, took him prisoner, and set up camp to await the arrival of the sheriff. Seizing upon a moment of laxity, Parker suddenly leapt forward, grabbed a

WOODCUT OF JIM PARKER PRIOR TO HIS EXECUTION

Winchester rifle, and pointed it at the deputy. Rogers retreated rapidly, and when Parker fired one shot, the Indians scattered into the brush and circled around to look for the sheriff while Parker escaped.

The next morning Sheriff Ruffner, with Deputies Buglin and Riley, started up Diamond Creek, searching for some sign of Parker. The party had not gone far when they saw the fugitive coming down the canyon, making his way toward the Grand Canyon. They set up a cross-fire ambush and waited. When Parker drew near, Ruffner called out, "Hands up!" Parker turned toward the sound, rifle at the ready, but the two deputies at his back repeated the same command. Parker looked over his shoulder and saw he was covered from all sides. Realizing that resistance was futile and probably fatal, he complied with the order and surrendered his Winchester.

The following day Parker arrived at Prescott and was lodged in jail. On February 24 he was taken before Justice J. M. W. Moore for his preliminary hearing and held for trial.

On Sunday, May 9, 1897, seven weeks before his trial, Parker escaped from the county jail with forger L. C. Miller and attempted murderer Cornelia Asarta. The fugitives were well armed and well mounted and had no trouble making a clean getaway. Prescott's *Daily Miner* reported:

DESPERATE JAIL BREAK THIS AFTERNOON

Lee Norris, who comes to Meador's Assistance, Shot Down by Parker with a Charge from a Shot Gun.

One of the most daring jail breaks ever attempted by desperate men was successfully made at 1 o'clock this afternoon from
the county jail. It was accomplished by the probable fatal wounding of Lee Norris, assistant district attorney of the county.

Lee Norris's wounds were not considered dangerous at first, as the shotgun was loaded with birdshot instead of buckshot. It soon became apparent, however, that Norris's condition would not stabilize. The evening of the escape, Norris developed alarming symptoms, according to the *Daily Miner,* and "he commenced having hemorrhages . . . when the physician pronounced his case hopeless, and he died just about midnight." Norris seemed to know from the first that his was a mortal wound, and he told this to friends and doctors, giving instructions for the disposition of his remains.

The charge against the fugitives was now murder, and rewards were offered accordingly. The governor issued a Proclamation of Reward in the amount of $500 each for Parker and Miller and $250 for Asarta. The county would add to those rewards, and later Wells, Fargo & Company would offer an additional $1,000 for Parker.

On Tuesday, May 18, Miller was captured at Jerome, Arizona Territory. On Wednesday, May 26, just at daybreak, Parker was captured about eighty miles north of Flagstaff. Cornelia Asarta was never found. Given the circumstances of the escape and subsequent events, it was likely that he died in the wilderness from the serious wound received during the jailbreak, from an infection, or from starvation or exposure.

While Parker awaited his trial for murder, Thompson was tried as an accessory to the train robbery and convicted. On June 28 he received a sentence of five and one-half years to be served in the territorial prison near Yuma.

Parker and Miller filed motions for separate trials on the murder charge, and also for a change of venue, but they were only granted separate trials. Miller was convicted of murder and sentenced to life in prison. He joined Thompson at the territorial prison on Sunday, July 4, 1897. Parker was convicted of murder in the first degree and sentenced to hang on August 14. Considering his death sentence, he was not tried for the train robbery as the cost of another trial could not be justified. After nearly a year of unsuccessful appeals, the new date for the execution was set for June 10, 1898.

On Wednesday, June 8, the day that work commenced on the eighteen-foot-high enclosure surrounding the gallows, Prescott's *Daily Miner* reported that while "in the scaffold's shadow," Parker was baptized into the Catholic Church. On Thursday evening the prisoner made preparations for his death. He asked for whiskey. He fell asleep at 4:00 A.M., but was awake at an early hour and ate a hearty breakfast.

At 10:00 A.M. on Friday, June 10, Sheriff Ruffner read the death warrant to Parker in his cell. Twenty-five minutes later they began the march to the scaffold. The sheriff had hold of Parker's left arm, while Deputy Jeff Davis was on his right. Parker's priest and Deputies J. P. Dillon and Pete Boscha, along with ex-deputy Johnny Munds, followed.

As Parker emerged from the gloom of the jail into the bright sunshine, his gaze rested on the gallows and he was visibly affected, faltering for just an instant. Quickly gathering his composure, Parker

Sharlot Hall Museum Photo, Prescott, Arizona

FLEMING PARKER AT HIS EXECUTION, ABOUT TO BE NOOSED

requested, "Hold on boys, I want to look at this thing; I never looked at one before." Sheriff Ruffner permitted him to go under the scaffold and examine it, and he spent several minutes seeming to be especially interested in the release mechanism for the trapdoor. After finishing his inspection, the prisoner ascended with a steady gait and stepped heavily upon the trapdoor, as if to test its strength.

Parker took off his slippers and threw them carelessly on the floor of the scaffold. While the condemned man was speaking to someone in the crowd, Sheriff Ruffner commenced buckling the straps around his legs. "Take your time, George," the prisoner said, "there is no use in putting them on; I am not going to straddle out; You needn't worry." After Parker's arms and legs had been pinioned, Deputy Dillon told him that if he had anything to say to the spectators, he could do so. Parker replied, "I have not much to say. I claim that I am getting something that ain't due me, but I guess every man who is about to be hanged says the same thing, so that don't cut no figure; whenever the people says I must go, I am one who can go, and make no kick."

The black cap was then drawn down over his face, but he said, "Hold on, I want to shake hands with the boys." The cap was removed and he shook hands with all those on the scaffold, saying that he had no ill feelings toward anyone. After shaking hands with everyone, he motioned to the jailer and shook hands with him a second time, holding his hand for a few seconds and remarking, "It's all off; tell the boys [meaning his fellow inmates] that I died game and like a man."

The black cap was again drawn over Parker's face, and Dillon adjusted the rope while Sheriff Ruffner stood with his hand poised on the lever of the trapdoor, preparing to spring it. Parker said to Dillon, "Don't get excited," and then to the sheriff, "George, you put her on." Dillon had the rope already adjusted properly, but the sheriff gave it a tug and at the same moment sprang the trap. Parker shot downward six feet, the whole thing done so quickly that the spectators could scarcely watch the movement. The trap was sprung at exactly 10:31 A.M., after which there were several convulsive twitches of the legs.

Doctors E. W. Dutcher and J. R. Walls were the official physicians in attendance, and they timed Parker's pulse. After ten minutes and fifty-four seconds, Parker was pronounced dead and the body was cut down. An examination showed that Parker's neck had been broken in the fall. When the black cap was removed, the features of the deceased appeared perfectly natural, with the exception of the open eyelids and a slightly drawn appearance to his mouth. The body was at once removed to Logan's Undertaking, where it was viewed by a large number of people during the afternoon. Parker was buried in Potter's Field at the expense of the county at 4:00 P.M.

Fleming "Jim" Parker was a cowboy bored by winter doldrums and looking for excitement. He started out to rob a train, but it ended with him murdering a leading citizen of Prescott, expiating this crime on the gallows.

A Hanging
Done Right

June 24, 1898

HERMAN ST. CLAIR, A MILITARY HERO AND ex-convict, was destitute in 1897, when he was befriended by John Decker in British Columbia. The two men started for Mexico, with Decker outfitting and paying for the entire trip. They only traveled as far as Idaho, however, when St. Clair betrayed and brutally murdered his benefactor. He was arrested and lodged in jail. When he tried to take "French leave," jailer James McQuillan intervened to stop the escape, and in the battle that followed, the prisoner was shot twice and stabbed fifteen times. By June 24, 1898, St. Clair had recovered sufficiently to expiate his crime on a trapdoor gallows.

Herman C. St. Clair (this was not his real name, but he would give no other) was born on October 4, 1849, in the capital of the Cherokee Nation Territory, present-day Oklahoma. He joined the U.S. Navy in 1864 and served until 1876. As soon as he was out of the navy, he enlisted as an Indian scout for the Army of the West and served with General George Crook on the Yellowstone survey. He was with General Nelson Miles when Sitting Bull's band was chased about the north-central part of the United States. In 1879 he was deployed to Idaho to serve under Colonel Reuben Bernard in the First Cavalry, Company G.

He was involved in several skirmishes with Indians, and at Deep Creek received a minor wound to his arm. During his military service he received three awards for bravery, but after mustering out, he went to California, where he became involved with sporting women, whiskey, and cards. This led him into a life of crime, and he served terms in California's Folsom and San Quentin Prisons under the alias Eugene St. Clair. When he was released from his last prison term, he went to British Columbia and met John Decker in 1896.

In October 1897, Decker and St. Clair started for Mexico in a wagon owned by Decker. Decker carried more than twelve hundred dollars in his belt and paid for everything they needed—St. Clair had no money. They traveled to Van Wyck in Long Valley, Idaho, and stayed Thursday night, October 21, in an abandoned cabin two miles from town.

The following day St. Clair went into Van Wyck alone, bringing a considerable amount of money, which he began to spend freely; he also began to drink heavily. He had a .38 caliber six-shooter that he tried to trade without success. When questioned about Decker, he said his companion had gone on to Boise on a freight train—though no trains had left Van Wyck recently. St. Clair's drunken debauchery continued into Saturday. With liquor loosening his tongue, he made several remarks regarding Decker that aroused suspicions of foul play .

Giving no indication that they were searching for Decker, a party of men went to the abandoned cabin on Sunday, October 24, while St. Clair was still in Van Wyck. At first there appeared to be no sign of Decker or of any struggle, but as the search widened, the party located a wagon track leading through the tall grass into a gulch. They followed the trail to where it ended and they found evidence that something heavy had been unloaded from the wagon bed and dragged through the grass.

Past the trail end two hundred yards, they found Decker's body wrapped in a blanket with double wrappings about the head. A rope around the dead man's neck had been used to drag the body. The search party left the body undisturbed, returned to Van Wyck, and arrested St. Clair, but they gave no clue as to the charge. They first took the prisoner to the cabin and then walked him up the gulch on a "search" for Decker. They allowed St. Clair to discover the body, carefully watching for any reaction that would give him away, but he showed only surprise. He recognized the body, but when accused of the murder, he protested that he was innocent. The party threatened lynching, which unnerved St. Clair, and though he made no confession, he made several conflicting statements that supported the belief that he was guilty. St. Clair was quickly taken to Idaho City by officers. As soon as he was out of danger of an extralegal hanging, he resumed his usual braggadocio.

St. Clair was examined, held for the grand jury, and indicted. The trial, which commenced on November 11, took seven days. The defendant refused to take the stand and would not allow his attorney, Karl Paine, to enter an insanity plea. On November 18, 1897, after a brief deliberation, the jury found St. Clair guilty of first-degree murder. Two days later the judge sentenced him to hang on January 14, 1898. On January 12 an appeal was filed with the Supreme Court, which served as a stay of execution. On May 10, the decision of the lower court was affirmed, and on June 14, 1898, St. Clair was sentenced to hang in ten days. The application for a commutation of sentence was denied.

During St. Clair's imprisonment, he tried to escape by sawing through a three-quarter-inch bar and sliding through the opening. He made his way to the rear door of the jail, and there the prisoner was confronted by jailer James McQuillan. St. Clair was armed with a knife and tried to take McQuillan's pistol, but he had seriously underestimated the jailer. McQuillan fought desperately to retain his gun, and St. Clair was shot through the jaw, breaking the bone and carrying away part of his tongue and several teeth. McQuillan wrestled St. Clair's knife from his grip, and in the ensuing struggle the prisoner was stabbed fifteen times. Nine wounds were quite deep and two penetrated the prisoner's lungs. St. Clair was so badly wounded that he had no choice but to give up. Even so, he survived his wounds.

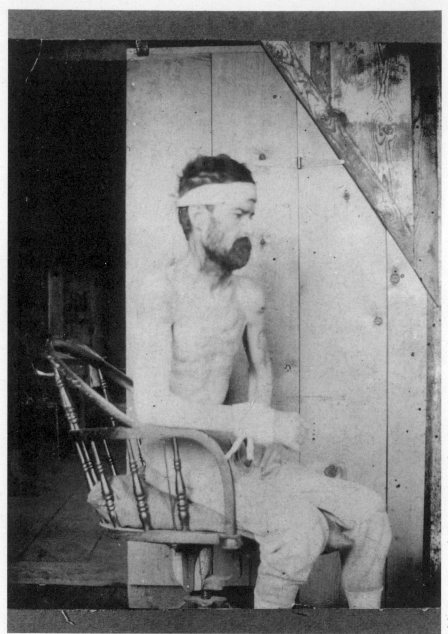

HERMAN ST. CLAIR IN 1898,
AWAITING HIS EXECUTION

As the fatal day approached, St. Clair continued to assert his innocence, but admitted he had buried Decker's money belt and most of his money near Joe Robbins's barn, "when I heard two men planning to rob Decker." He said he thought the money might still be there and suggested that these two unnamed men had probably gone through with their plan and killed Decker while trying to learn where the money was hidden. This explanation was dismissed as implausible.

St. Clair refused to name the person who had aided in his escape attempt by providing the file and knife; likewise, he would not provide any names and addresses of relatives so they could be contacted. He told Guy Flenner, the reporter for the Boise, Idaho, *Statesman*, that philosophically he looked forward to his fate, and said:

> I am losing no sleep. No use to worry now; I might as well laugh as cry; my fate is fixed and there is no way to avoid it. I am a fatalist and believe that whatever is to be. I intend to perform my part next Friday. Being so weak I don't think I will be able to walk up the steps of the scaffold without assistance. If I was not to be hanged I could not go up without being helped, or at any rate I would have to go very slowly and stop to rest more than once before reaching the top.

He said that if his fate were not to hang, he would soon die from infection in his jaw wound anyway, and showed the reporter that the cut to his wrist had severed the cords and left his hand misshapen and his fingers useless. His form, "once sturdy as an oak, was emaciated," according to Flenner, "and his step was feeble. Irregular whiskers about two inches long covered his face, which was pale as death in contrast to his red whiskers. He looked like a walking corpse."

A week before the execution, the invitation was sent to a number of witnesses and read:

Idaho City, Boise County, Idaho.
June 15th 1898.
Mr.____. You are requested to be
present at the execution of
H. C. St. Clair on June 24th, 1898
at 10 A.M. at Idaho City, Idaho
                    J. A. Lippincott
                        Sheriff

The prisoner slept little his last night, finally dozing off at 12:30 A.M., but waking at 2:00. He again fell asleep after 6:00 and had to be awakened at 9:30 for breakfast in the jail corridor. To accommodate his shattered jaw, he ate a hearty meal of soft items, which included poached eggs, minced meat, strawberries, and cream. He appeared calm and composed when he returned to his cell after breakfast, and he began dressing in a new suit of clothes. At 10:10 A.M. Dr. Warren Newell of Idaho City, Dr. A. C. Lippincott of Boise, and Dr. E. E. Maxey of Caldwell examined the prisoner and found his pulse at 106, but it was reduced to 96 in five minutes by the administration of a whiskey toddy and a small dose of morphine. The prisoner then asked for a little more time. He was granted eight minutes. At 10:23 Sheriff Lippincott announced that the time had arrived, and St. Clair grabbed his vest and coat, stepped out of his cell, and finished dressing in the corridor.

Deputy McQuillan, Elder Smith, and Clay Mosher applied the straps to St. Clair's arms, and the prisoner carefully smoothed out his clothing while they worked. When the chest strap was secured, he complained, "That's too tight, old man; I want it so I can breathe good." When they were done, he examined the work and announced, "Why, that's good enough for anybody."

Sheriff Lippincott was beside the prisoner with one deputy in front and two behind as they walked to the gallows. At the scaffold the

ST. CLAIR'S GALLOWS

Idaho State Historical Society, 62-14.20

deputies offered assistance in climbing the stairs, but St. Clair declined, saying, "Never mind. I can walk up there." He ascended the thirteen steps and stood on the trapdoor facing east. Mosher touched St. Clair's shoulder, as he was preoccupied looking at the scene, and he turned his head to accommodate adjustment of the noose. Mosher cinched the noose, which had been obtained by the sheriff from California's San Quentin prison along with the black cap. St. Clair complained that the noose was too tight, and it was loosened slightly.

The prisoner glanced over the crowd, as if preparing to make a speech, but finally spied Guy Flenner, the *Statesman* reporter, and said, "Good-bye, old man; take good care of yourself." Mosher then pulled on the black cap. The condemned man spoke his final words, a muffled "Good-bye, everybody!" The sheriff and Deputy Smith each stood at a lever, one of which was a dummy. When Mosher waved his hand, the trap was sprung and the prisoner fell six feet. The three doctors immediately attended the dangling man and reported that they felt no pulse at thirty-eight seconds, but continued to monitor him for possible vital signs until they pronounced life extinct in eight minutes.

St. Clair's neck had been broken by the fall, and there was neither a quiver nor a convulsive movement detected. The body was cut down and carried into the jail, where a casket awaited the murderer's remains. When the cap was removed, it was found that the rope had cut through the skin, but most of the blood had come from the jaw wound, which had been reopened by the drop. The prisoner had protested an autopsy, but one was performed. When his brain was removed some features of abnormality were discovered, though not described by the doctors. Fifteen knife wounds were found on his body and two bullet wounds, as well as a number of tattoos acquired while in prison.

The undertaker then took charge of the remains, and that afternoon Herman St. Clair was buried on the hill near the city cemetery, next to the grave of murderer Simeon Walters, hanged December 10, 1869. The painted wooden grave marker bore the simple inscription: H. C. St. Clair. Hanged June 24, 1898, for the murder of John Decker.

Beheaded
by the Noose

April 25, 1901

THOMAS EDWARD KETCHUM WAS MISTAKENLY saddled with the sobriquet "Black Jack." Even Ketchum, after he was captured, did all he could to discourage its use, but the misnaming has persisted for over a century. Tom Ketchum's notoriety comes not from his nickname, however, but from two interesting developments related to his death: first, Thomas was the only man on America's western frontier legally executed for a crime other than first-degree murder; and second, his execution was the most bungled affair in the annals of frontier justice.

In 1849 Peter Ketchum led two wagon trains into Texas, where the Ketchum families established cattle ranches. Green Ketchum, Peter's oldest son, came from Illinois with his wife Temperance. The couple had five children—Elizabeth, Green Jr., Samuel, Nancy B., and Tom, born on Halloween Day in 1863. In his youth Tom had minor skirmishes with the law like many boys his age. As young men, Tom and his brother Sam— the Ketchum boys—worked at various ranches from Texas to Wyoming and became close friends with William R. Carver and David Atkins.

Carver was born in Comanche County, Texas, in September 1868, and after his father abandoned his family, they moved to Pipe

Creek in Bandera County. There Carver was introduced to the cowboy life by Uncle Dick Carver. David Atkins was a native of Tom Green County and met the Ketchums when they moved there in the early 1880s. He married Saba Banner in 1894, and soon after they had a baby girl. Before long Atkins abandoned his family to join Carver and the Ketchum boys in a life of crime.

In 1895 Ketchum's neighbors, the Powers, were having serious marital problems. Mrs. John N. "Jap" Powers was looking for a way to be rid of her husband. On December 12, "Jap" was brutally murdered. He was shot in the back three times and the coup de grace was inflicted to his head from close range. Tom Ketchum, David Atkins, and another man were eventually indicted, but they had already fled from Texas into New Mexico Territory. The following year the sheriff insisted that the three men were innocent and declared that he would not pursue them further, as "Jap" Power's wife and another man had become the focus of his investigation.

In the meantime the Ketchum boys were working on the Bell ranch in New Mexico Territory. When Sam had a dispute with the ranch foreman, the boys left, but soon returned to steal supplies from the Bell storehouse. This was the first crime attributed to the Ketchum boys acting together, and it was followed quickly by a burglary of the post office and store at Liberty, New Mexico. One of the owners of the store, Levi Herzstein, and Merejildo Gallegos, a leading Mexican citizen often used as an interpreter, pursued the Ketchums. In the pursuit they were shot to death. To avoid a murder charge, Sam and Tom fled into Arizona Territory, where they joined Carver and Atkins in Graham County.

In 1897 Tom Ketchum, Carver, and Atkins headed south to Lozier, Texas, a water stop on the Galveston, Harrisburg & San Antonio Railroad. Just before 2:00 A.M. on May 14, Tom and Carver climbed over the tender, pointed their six-shooters at engineer George Freese and fireman James Bochat, and took control of the train. They stopped the engine at the next cut, where Atkins had severed the telegraph wires and was

Black Jack Ketchum,--photo made just
before his execution at Clayton,
New Mexico, April 1, 1901.

THOMAS KETCHUM, JUST BEFORE HIS EXECUTION

waiting with horses and explosives. The three men entered the express car, took agent W. H. Joyce prisoner, and blew open the way safe. They then took three sacks of plunder valued at forty-two-thousand dollars. Several posses were soon in the field, but the three train robbers managed to elude capture and made their way to Tom Green County, where they spent nearly all they had stolen bribing the locals to hide and feed them.

When their money ran low, the boys decided they should rob another train, this time in New Mexico. The fact that New Mexico Territory had made train robbery a capital offense in 1887 did not deter them. Tom was joined by brother Sam, while Carver and Atkins enlisted the help of a fifth man named Charles Collings, and the party of five made their way to the Twin Mountains bend, between Folsom and Des Moines, New Mexico.

On September 3, 1897, they stopped the southbound No. 1 Gulf, Colorado & Santa Fe Railroad train, and messenger Charles F. Drew was brutally assaulted by Sam Ketchum. It took three charges to blow the safe, and they found inside less than three thousand five hundred dollars in money, some assorted jewelry, and other small items. The gang hid for several days in Turkey Creek Canyon near Cimarron, New Mexico Territory, and then headed for the southeastern corner of Arizona Territory, where they began planning their next robbery. A man by the name of Bruce "Red" Weaver was falsely arrested and tried for the crime, but there was little evidence to tie him to the robbery and he was acquitted.

Deputy U.S. marshals had not been able to find the robbers, but in late November 1897, they received word that a train would be robbed at Stein's Pass near the border between New Mexico and Arizona in early December. On December 9, Atkins and the newest gang member Ed Cullen robbed Stein's post office. For all of their effort, the haul was only nine dollars. After the robbery, the two men joined Tom Ketchum at the depot for the next crime. They searched the offices of the express company at the Stein's Pass station, where they found a little more than two dollars and a Winchester .44 caliber rifle.

Next on the agenda was the Stein's Pass train robbery. Tom Ketchum and Carver rode their horses two miles farther west and built signal fires on both sides of the tracks at a point where there was a steep grade. The westbound No. 20 train came along at 9:00 P.M., and Atkins and Cullen forced agent Charles St. John to show a red warning light— a signal of danger ahead that indicated the engineer was to stop the train. They boarded the engine and captured engineer Thomas W. North and his fireman, then required North to pull ahead to the signal fires. Once the train was in position, the robbers approached the express car, but messenger Charles Jennings and two other guards began firing at them. Four robbers were wounded, Cullen was killed, and the gang was forced to flee, leaving Cullen's body behind.

After another failed endeavor, the gang was still broke and anxious to secure another large haul. They returned to familiar territory near Lozier, Texas, and this time set their sights on the Comstock station on the Galveston, Harrisburg & San Antonio Railroad, halfway between Langtry and Del Rio.

On April 28, 1898, at 11:30 P.M., the westbound No. 20 was leaving the station when two armed men, carefully masked, climbed over the tender and captured engineer Walter Jordan and his fireman. They ordered him to stop the train, and as soon as it came to a halt, two men appeared and uncoupled the passenger cars from the rear of the express car. They forced Jordan to take the remainder of the train, consisting of the engine, tender, and express car, westward to Helmet before they stopped the train again and approached the express car. Messenger Richard Hayes was about to make a fight of it when a cartridge jammed in his Winchester rifle and he had to surrender. The robbers cleaned out the safes and took an estimated twenty thousand dollars. It was seven hours before a posse could take to the field. Once they did, however, they returned to town empty-handed, with no further clues or tracks to follow.

The Ketchum gang decided that on their next job they would try the same ruse they had used unsuccessfully at Stein's Pass—displaying a red warning light. They moved north to Mustang Creek, Texas, and on July 1, 1898, they stopped the westbound Texas Pacific No. 3 train, threw a switch, and directed the train onto a siding. The passenger cars were uncoupled and the engine, tender, and express car were pulled ahead a safe distance to prevent interference. The men easily gained entrance to the express car and blew the safe with explosives. They took out an estimated fifty thousand dollars, leaving behind a large number of ten-dollar bills and assorted jewelry. The gang escaped again.

In the spring of 1899, the Ketchum brothers quarreled and Sam Ketchum and Carver split from Tom. Sam formed a new gang, and together they planned a repeat robbery at Twin Mountains, taking in the Colorado & Southern Railway. The attack was successful and the men made their getaway, but a posse soon caught up to them. In the ensuing battle Sam Ketchum was mortally wounded; he died of an infection on July 24, 1899.

After splitting from his brother, Tom went to Prescott, Arizona, where on July 2, he murdered two men. Tom had heard nothing of the train robbery, the shoot-out, or the death of his brother; he had spent July on the trail, heading toward New Mexico. He planned to reconcile with Sam and decided that it was time to execute their plans to repeat the robbery at Twin Mountains, not knowing Sam had already done this. When he was unable to find his brother, Carver, or any other gang member, Tom decided to try the train robbery alone. He abandoned his attempt on August 11, when he saw an armed guard in the express car. He then anxiously made his way to Folsom.

On August 16 at 10:20 P.M., a solo Tom Ketchum climbed aboard the blind baggage—the platform on the front of the express car—of the southbound No. 1 Colorado & Southern Railway train when it stopped at Folsom to take on water. With his Winchester rifle, Tom captured engineer Joseph Kirchgrabber and had him stop the train at the bend four miles south of the station, two miles from the place Tom had tied his horse. In the express car was Charles Drew, the messenger who had

KETCHUM ON THE GALLOWS,
BEING PREPARED FOR THE DROP

been badly beaten by Sam Ketchum in 1897, and in his care was over $5,000.

Tom ordered Drew out of the car and had him hold a lantern while the fireman tried to unlock the couplings behind the express car. Instead the fireman cut the air hoses, which locked the brakes on all the cars. Fred Bartlett, the mail clerk, stuck his head out to see what was happening, and Tom, an excellent marksman, fired a warning shot. The bullet ricocheted and struck Bartlett in the jaw, causing a serious, but not fatal, wound. The fireman then said he had uncoupled the cars, but he had not, so Tom ordered the engineer to finish the task.

While Kirchgrabber struggled with the coupling, conductor Frank Harrington, who had been defenseless during an earlier Ketchum gang robbery, opened the door to the first coach behind the express car and discharged his shotgun at Tom. The heavy load of buckshot tore a gaping wound in the robber's right arm, just above the elbow. Tom tried to shoot Harrington when he first appeared, but Tom's shot went wild when he was struck by Harrington's buckshot.

Tom stumbled off into the darkness and sent a couple of shots toward the lantern, to discourage anyone from following. He managed to make it to his horse, but he had already lost so much blood that he was too weak to mount. He lay down beside the tracks and waited. The following day the posse arrived, found the wounded robber in his weakened condition, and easily captured Tom Ketchum.

Tom was indicted and tried on the Federal charge of assault on a U.S. mail agent, and he was sentenced to a ten-year prison term. While he was being held at the prison, his wounded arm became so infected that it had to be amputated. The following year Tom was tried again for the same robbery, but this time on the Territorial charge of "assault upon a railroad train with intent to commit a felony," a capital offense. He was convicted and became the first person sentenced to hang for assaulting a train.

As the date for his execution approached, he was taken to Clayton in Union County and lodged in their jail. From his window, he was able to see the carpenters constructing the gallows and the high-board fence around it as required by law. He complimented them on their skill. As his one last request he asked for female company, but this was denied as there were no funds authorized to pay for a "lady of the town."

A priest came from Trinidad, New Mexico, and stayed with the condemned man throughout his last night. In the morning the prisoner ate a hearty breakfast, then washed and dressed in the new suit provided by Sheriff Salome Garcia. After the death warrant was read, he seemed anxious to proceed, but it was still too early. At 11:30 A.M. he asked for music, and a violinist and a guitarist played as he ate his dinner. At 12:30 P.M. he named all those involved in his prosecution and promised that they were marked for death by members of his gang.

Denver Public Library, Western History Collection, #F-9484

KETCHUM, BEHEADED BY THE NOOSE,
BENEATH THE GALLOWS

At 1:15 P.M. Tom Ketchum began his march to the gallows accompanied by the priest, with the sheriff on his right and witness Harry Lewis of Trinidad on his left. The condemned man climbed the stairs with a firm step and his head down, and took his place upon the trapdoor. His arm and legs were pinioned, the noose adjusted, and the black cap pulled over his head. He had declined to make a speech, but when there was a brief delay, he called out, "Let 'er go, boys!"

Governor Otero had sent a man to oversee the preparations and ensure that everything went smoothly. The drop had been calculated at five-feet-nine inches, a few inches longer than required for a man near two hundred pounds. The governor's man, however, had increased the length of the drop, and at the last minute Sheriff Garcia, concerned the drop still might not do the trick, increased it to seven feet. The hangman's rope had been carefully soaked and stretched with a heavy weight to remove elasticity. The stretching had made the rope, already a bit thin for a hanging, almost cordlike. Where fiber crossed fiber, it was lubricated with soap to ensure the knot would slide easily. Another piece of rope was used to secure the trapdoor, and the trap was sprung by cutting this rope.

When the moment arrived the sheriff cut the trapdoor rope with a single stroke and Tom Ketchum's body shot downward. The thin rope cut through the condemned's neck and spine, severing Ketchum's head from his body, and both fell to the ground. Blood spurted from the torso's neck. The head, in its black bag, rolled about beneath the gallows, while the bloody rope rebounded high into the air.

After photographers were done with their grisly work documenting the worst bungled execution in the history of the western frontier, the head and torso were collected by the undertaker and the head was sewn back on. Thomas Ketchum was buried in the town's cemetery the following day.

The rest of the Ketchum gang continued on, for a time anyway. Carver joined the Wild Bunch and was eventually shot dead in Sonora, Texas, on April 2, 1901. Atkins was arrested in March of 1900 and returned to Texas, where he jumped bail and fled to England. He was finally captured in 1911 during a visit to Tom Green County, Texas. He was sentenced to serve five years for an earlier murder, but not for any of his crimes with the Ketchum boys. He died in 1964 after spending his last three decades in an insane asylum. Tom Ketchum, however, had long since paid for his crimes, dying in the most brutal manner imaginable, by being hanged and subsequently beheaded.

The Last Hanging
in Prescott, Arizona

July 31, 1903

FRANCISCO RENTARIO HELD A GRUDGE against Charles Goddard for two years before returning to Goddard, Arizona Territory. With the help of Hilario Hidalgo, he settled the grudge by murdering his nemesis and an innocent bystander. It took some time to track the two fugitives into Mexico using ingenious plans to lure them back onto American soil where they could be arrested. Once Rentario and Hidalgo were finally apprehended, the two men were sentenced to hang at Prescott in Yavapai County, and on July 31, 1903, both murderers were simultaneously dropped to their deaths. They were the last men hanged on the courthouse plaza at Prescott.

Goddard, Arizona, was named after the Goddard family, who owned a successful sheep ranch in the vicinity. Each year during the sheep-shearing season, Charles Goddard hired extra help. In mid-February 1901 he hired a troublesome Mexican named Francisco Rentario (sometimes spelled Renteria or Rentezia). When a dispute arose between Rentario and another shearer, Rentario tried to stab his fellow worker with his shears. Goddard intervened and struck Rentario across the face with his six-shooter. The barrel of the gun caused a deep gash and knocked him to the ground. When Rentario recovered, it was clear that the gash would leave a large scar. Rentario swore loudly and openly that he would kill Charles Goddard for preventing his attack on his coworker and for the serious wound and scar. However, Goddard soon forgot the incident, as he had many thousands of sheep to shear and was much too busy to be distracted for long. When the season ended, Rentario left without further incident. He did not appear for employment at the Goddard farm during the 1902 season.

On February 1, 1903, as the shearing season was about to begin again, two hard cases arrived from the Prescott area and hung around Goddard's two-story building, which served as headquarters for his sheep ranching enterprise. The two men approached Francisco Rodriguez, who managed the ranch, and several times asked a variety of questions about the forthcoming shearing season. They inquired about when the other shearers would arrive, if the payroll had been brought in, and asked general questions about the Goddards and others at the station. The two men continued to lurk around the ranch even after asking all their questions.

That evening Charles and Rosa Goddard sat down to their Sunday supper with Frank Cox (sometimes spelled Cocke), who ran the on-site post office, and an overnight guest named Milton Turnbull. Rosa was just going to the kitchen when the two sketchy men, both heavyset, suddenly burst into the room and demanded food. Charles explained that the meal was finished, but told the men if they would wait, some food would be prepared for them. One of the men shouted, "No! Now!" and both men immediately drew their six-shooters and fired upon Goddard, Cox, and Turnbull.

Frank Cox was killed immediately, while Charles Goddard received several mortal wounds to his chest and fell to the floor, bleeding. A bullet hit Turnbull's chair, and he fell over and feigned death. Rosa, upon hearing the noise, ran upstairs and hid. The two murderers then ate what they could find on the table and in the kitchen, and ransacked the first floor, looking for a payroll. Luckily for Rosa, they did not go upstairs. They discussed what to do next and then blew out all the lamps and fled. Turnbull lay still until daylight, afraid to light a lamp in case the men should return to finish their murderous work. Rosa remained upstairs the entire time, hidden and also afraid the men might return. By morning Charles Goddard had bled to death.

At dawn Turnbull finally felt brave enough and saddled a horse and rode to the Cordes Ranch. Turnbull explained the events of the night before and a rider from the ranch continued on to the railroad depot at Mayer to report the incident. A telegram was sent to Deputy Sheriff Joseph Campbell at Prescott, and he forwarded the message to Sheriff Joe Roberts, who was in Phoenix. Sheriff Campbell then made the trip to Goddard, picking up Deputy George Heisler along the way. Rosa Goddard and Francisco Rodriguez gave excellent descriptions of the two fugitives. Rodriguez said the man with the scar looked familiar; he later recalled the incident that had taken place two years earlier and informed Sheriff Roberts about it, but he couldn't remember Rentario's name. The sheriff was afraid he would lose contact with this valuable witness if Rodriguez moved on after the shearing season, so he gave him work on his ranch near Prescott.

The deputies looked for the fugitives' trail, but it had been washed away by recent heavy rainstorms. With no further leads they decided to wait for someone to provide them with information on the murderers.

Meanwhile, Rosa Goddard boarded the southbound stage and rode to Phoenix, where her children were in school. The driver heard the details of the murders from Rosa and remembered seeing two men who matched the fugitives' descriptions walking southward when he had come up on Monday. He reported this to the sheriff.

An indictment was returned by the grand jury, with the names Richard Roe and John Doe, and descriptive circulars were sent throughout the territory, especially along the U.S.–Mexico border. Soon leads were coming in. One of the first was from Frank Murphy, a railroad promoter, who came into the sheriff's office in Prescott to report that two troublemakers had been fired by the railroad on the Friday before the murders. They fit the descriptions being circulated. Murphy provided their names: Hilario Hidalgo from Chihuahua, Mexico, and Francisco Rentario from Guanajato, Mexico. Two days later Sheriff Adelbert Lewis of Cochise County notified Deputy Heisler that the two men he was seeking were working in Naco, a border town south of Bisbee. When Heisler arrived, however, Naco Deputy Billy Blankenship told him that the men were actually working in Mexico.

Hidalgo was employed on a section crew for the Southern Pacific Railroad, laying tracks into Mexico, while Rentario was working at a mine several miles below the border. Relations with Mexico were poor at the time, and there were no extradition arrangements with the Mexican authorities. The border was poorly marked and everyone, except lawmen and the militaries of the two countries, passed back and forth freely. Deputies Blankenship and Heisler met with the manager of the railroad and arranged for Hidalgo's section crew to work on the tracks north of the border. Hidalgo, when approached by the lawmen, believed he was still in Mexico and surrendered without resistance, confident he could easily avoid extradition. He was lodged in the jail at Naco to await the arrest of Rentario.

The deputies had a plan to capture Rentario. They met with the mine manager and arranged for him to pay his crew with drafts drawn on a bank just over the international border in Naco. Cautiously, Rentario went to the bank on an April morning, but the bank was closed and he ran back into Mexico. Later in the day, when a fellow miner signaled that the coast was clear, Rentario again crossed into the United States and was immediately arrested.

On April 6, 1903, the prisoners were taken to Prescott and lodged in the Yavapai County Jail, which was located in the basement of the courthouse. On June 2 the two defendants—under the names on the indictment, Richard Roe and John Doe—pled not guilty and trial was set for June 10. Defense attorneys C. N. Hicks and Leroy Anderson were appointed to the case. The trial was held in the district court at Prescott, and both Rosa Goddard and Francisco Rodriguez positively identified the two defendants as the murderers. There were only seven witnesses for the prosecution, and although the two men produced several alibi witnesses, they were both found guilty of first-degree murder after only thirty minutes of deliberation.

The condemned men failed to file an appeal, and so the administration of capital punishment in this case was swift. Within a week the defendants were brought into court and sentenced to hang on July 31, 1903. On July 27 the building of the gallows commenced on the east side of the courthouse. As required by Arizona law at the time, the area around the gallows was walled off by a high wooden fence, and only those invited as witnesses would be permitted entry. Sheriff Roberts sent out invitations well in advance of the date. They were worded very cautiously, given the criticism and embarrassment suffered by Sheriff F. J. Wattron of Navajo County when he hanged George Smiley on January 8, 1900. Wattron's invitation had been characterized as "flippant," and had received attention from newspapers worldwide, so this invitation read:

> With feelings of profound regret and sorrow, I hereby invite you to attend and witness the private and decent and humane execution of two human beings, namely: Richard Roe and John Doe. Crime—Murder.
>
> Said men will be executed on July 31, 1903 at 12 noon. You are expected to deport yourself in a respectful manner and any flippant or unseemly language or conduct on your part will not be allowed. Conduct on anyone's part bordering on ribaldry and tending to mar the solemnity of the occasion will not be tolerated.

EXECUTION OF MEXICAN MURDERERS
No. 3.   PRESCOTT, ARIZ. 1904.

BRISLEY
DRUG CO.

HILARIO HIDALGO AND FRANCISCO RENTARIO
MOMENTS AFTER THEIR HANGING

On the morning of July 31, Sheriff Roberts, with a reporter from Prescott's *Journal Miner* as a witness, read the death warrant to each man in his cell. Hidalgo laughed and said that he had heard it many times before, at the preliminary examination, the indictment, the trial, and the sentencing. "If that were a song," he said, "I could sing it to you now."

Rentario asked the sheriff to let two other prisoners witness the execution, and the sheriff granted this request. A priest then administered the last rites to the condemned men and prayed with them until the time approached to march to the gallows. The condemned men bathed, shaved, and dressed in the new black suits provided by the sheriff. They were escorted up the stairs from the basement jail into the fenced enclosure, and with a firm step they walked up the thirteen steps to the scaffold at 11:15 A.M., with the priest leading the way.

Hidalgo was placed on the north trapdoor and Rentario on the south. As Hidalgo's arms and legs were being pinioned, he noticed some acquaintances in the crowd of five hundred spectators. Calling to them by name, he made some remarks in Spanish that were not recorded by the press. Rentario also spoke to several people in the crowd. Hidalgo was game to the last, but Rentario was betrayed by trembling and regret. Just as the black cap was pulled over their heads, they both shouted, "Adios! Adios todos!" and then Hidalgo said, muffled somewhat by the hood, "Good-bye, Frank" to the man who had sat the deathwatch with them for the past week.

The trap was sprung by Sheriff Roberts at 11:24 A.M. Hidalgo's neck was broken; Rentario died by strangulation. Both men were pronounced dead by the attending physicians ten minutes and forty seconds after they were dropped. They were buried in Potter's Field at county expense that evening.

Hidalgo and Rentario were hardened criminals and they paid for their crimes. Theirs was the last hanging in Prescott. The legislature soon removed the responsibility for legal executions from the sheriff of each county and placed it with the warden at the new prison in Florence.

The Hanging of an Innocent Man?

November 20, 1903

THOMAS HORN WAS AN AMERICAN LEGEND who sealed his own fate through liquor-induced braggadocio. He was surely responsible for several murders of suspected rustlers while working as a range detective, a mild term used to describe a paid assassin. But he may have been innocent of the crime for which he was sentenced to die: the murder of fourteen-year-old Willie Nickell. After Horn's conviction, his appeals were the most aggressive ones ever conducted on the frontier, but it was all to no avail. Horn was hanged in Cheyenne, Wyoming, on November 20, 1903, showing perhaps more courage than any other man on the scaffold.

Tom Horn was born into a large family in Franklin County, Missouri, in 1870. While he was a youngster, his father was a fugitive of the law for the crime of forgery. Tom left home and drifted to the southwest, making his living driving bull teams into Texas and New Mexico. He earned a reputation for himself when he killed a Mexican army officer over the affections of a girl. In New Mexico, Horn reportedly killed two sheepherders, but the law could never make the case and he was never arrested. While in New Mexico he joined the army as a scout and once fought off a gang of Mexicans and Indians single-handedly until his posse could rally to support him. As a scout he became close friends with Colonel W. F. "Buffalo Bill" Cody and General Nelson A. Miles.

Eventually he took a position as a cattle detective in Wyoming, where he rode the range, intent on stopping the rustlers. In that year William Powell and William Lewis were murdered at their small ranches forty-five miles north of Cheyenne when both were suspected of rustling. Every effort was made to work up the case against Horn, but it was without success.

In 1898 Horn enlisted in the government's pack-train service and went to Cuba during the Spanish-American War. He caught yellow fever soon after arriving there. When he returned to the states, it took him some months to regain his health.

On June 2, 1899, six robbers held up the Union Pacific train one mile west of Wilcox, Wyoming. Horn had recovered enough by then to take the trail and hunt down the robbers. Some time after the robbery, he returned to Wilcox and claimed four thousand dollars of the reward for killing two of the robbers, whom he buried where they had fallen. He was not believed, however, and so he led officers to the spot and dug up the remains. The evidence showed that the two men he had killed were harmless prospectors whom he had shot from ambush without warning. He was denied reward money and thereafter referred to that incident as his "funny mistake," but yet he was not arrested for murdering two innocent victims.

In 1900 Matt Rash and Isham Dart, small ranchers in Brown's Hole County, Colorado, were assassinated. Both men had been suspected of rustling cattle, and it happened that Horn was in the county when they were killed. He even ate supper with Dart the night before his death. A posse went out after Horn and actually crossed his path, but they did not recognize him. He rode easily into Wyoming. At Dixon he stopped for a drink and became involved in an altercation with one

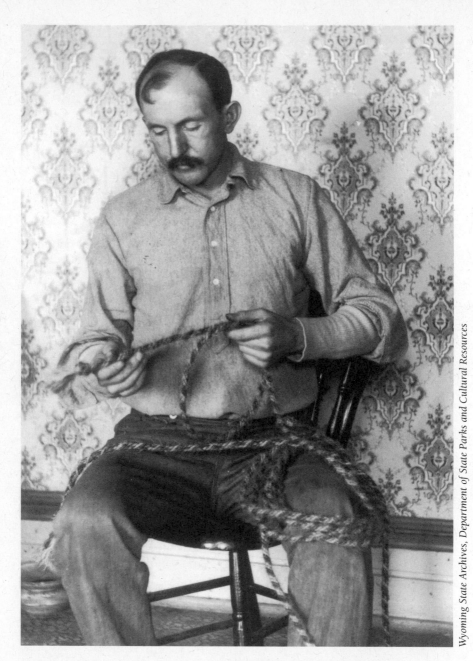

TOM HORN BRAIDING ROPE AS HE AWAITS HIS EXECUTION

of the posse members. He was cut severely on the back of his neck and the wound scarred noticeably.

As soon as Horn was back in Wyoming, he was employed as a range detective for the Iron Mountain Ranch Company, which operated ranches at Bosler in Albany County and Iron Mountain in Laramie County. About this time there was a feud between the Miller family and the Nickell family in the Iron Mountain district, because Kels P. Nickell had brought sheep into cattle country. At 7:00 in the morning, on July 18, 1901, Willie Nickell, the fourteen-year-old son of Kels, was near the ranch wearing his father's coat and hat when he was shot in the back twice. He died instantly, and at first, the Millers were suspected. Three weeks later Kels Nickell was shot, but managed to get into his house before being killed. He was taken to Cheyenne for treatment and recovered. He accused the Millers of the shooting. However, Jim and his sixteen-year-old son had an alibi and were released.

Horn was seen in the vicinity a few days before Willie Nickell was murdered, but could not be found after the killing. He finally turned up at the Bosler ranch and consented to testify regarding his innocence at the inquest. He told of his whereabouts and the coroner's jury again had to adjourn without a verdict.

Horn had a habit of drinking too much, and when inebriated, he laid claim to just about every unsolved murder and other outrageous act he could remember. Despite his drunken confessions, few people took his boasting seriously.

U.S. Marshal Joe Lafors had been assigned to investigate the murder of Willie Nickell. He soon became convinced that Horn was responsible. In December, Lafors had a friend write to Horn, offering him a position in Montana, which required him to go to Cheyenne and meet with Lafors to make the arrangements.

On January 12, 1902, Horn had been drinking heavily when he went to the Lafors's office. While further plying Horn with liquor, the detective got him to confess to the murder of the Nickell boy and got

HORN'S JURY

an admission to the killing of Powell and Lewis in 1894. It's uncertain whether the confessions were genuine or more braggadocio—Lafors didn't care either way. In the next room were two witnesses, Deputy Sheriff Les Snow and stenographer Charles Ohnhaus, who recorded the entire conversation. The following day Horn was arrested by Sheriff Edward J. Smalley and Undersheriff Richard A. Proctor.

Horn had his preliminary hearing in February, and his trial was set for the May term of the district court, but his attorneys obtained a delay to the fall term. Horn's trial began on October 24, 1902, and after thirteen days of testimony, the jury found him guilty of first-degree murder. A few days later Horn was sentenced to hang on January 9, 1903.

Then began one of the most aggressive appeals processes ever conducted. The execution was stayed as it took almost a year for the Supreme Court to consider the facts before affirming the lower court's decision. In October they rescheduled the execution of Horn for

November 20, 1903. The fight for Horn's life next went to the governor, where the state's executive was inundated with affidavits from both sides and testimony of every sort. He even received a letter from a dying man, who said he was guilty of the murder and would confess on his deathbed.

On November 15 Governor Fenimore Chatterton refused to interfere. There were many rumors that the jail would be infiltrated by sympathizers and Horn would be rescued, but the only incident that materialized was Horn's escape in August 1903. He only traveled two hundred yards before he was recaptured and wounded slightly. He had armed himself with an automatic pistol that he acquired in the Sheriff's office, but he had not learned how to release the safety. Unable to return fire, he had no choice but to surrender.

On Horn's last night he slept soundly and arose in excellent spirits. He asked for writing materials and spent the morning writing farewell letters, except for the few minutes he spent with his religious advisor, Reverend G. C. Rafter, and with his friend, John C. Coble. He ate a hearty breakfast and enjoyed several cigars as he whiled away the last hours. He dressed in a red-striped shirt with a low collar, a corduroy vest, black trousers, and gaiters.

At 9:00 A.M. the number of militiamen guarding the jail was greatly increased, and they formed a cordon around the building to keep back the growing crowd. Many of the spectators had taken up places in windows and on rooftops, but they could see nothing of the scaffold, which had been designed by Cheyenne architect James P. Julian. At 9:45 a final test of the gallows was conducted and everything worked efficiently. The hearse from Gleason's Undertaking Parlor stood near the courthouse and attracted much attention from the crowd. At 10:55 the invited witnesses were admitted and began filing into the enclosure.

Horn was brought out as far as the gangway, where he stopped while Frank and Charlie Irwin sang a tune, a strange medley of railroad vernacular and sacred words. The two boys were summoned to the scaffold and they shook hands with Horn and told him to die game. Charlie Irwin asked Horn if he had confessed, and the condemned man said, in a most emphatic tone of voice, "No!"

When the singers left the platform, Deputy Sheriff Proctor secured the straps about Horn's wrists and thighs and the condemned man joked with those in his procession. He was led onto the platform, where he examined the trapdoor carefully and remarked, "I never saw one just like that before. I've seen several of them, but that is a new one."

At 11:04 A.M. the noose was put over his head and Horn bent forward to help Proctor get it in place easily. His knees and ankles were then bound, and as the straps were cinched tight, he was jerked about and said, "You're liable to tip me over here; somebody had better hold me. You fellows ought to have a handle on me so you could do this easier."

Reverend Rafter read a short passage from an Episcopal prayer book. As the reverend spoke, Horn moved his head about as if the rope were uncomfortable, so Proctor stepped forward and lifted the heavy hangman's knot off Horn's shoulder. While in that position, Horn inspected the details of the knot.

When the prayer finished at 11:06, Proctor lowered the knot into place and pulled the black cap over Horn's smiling face. The deputy asked, "Are you ready, Tom?" and he replied, "Yes!" Sheriff Smalley and Joe Cahill lifted the condemned man onto the trapdoor. As he was being lifted, he said, "Ain't gettin' nervous, are you?" and laughed through the cap. As soon as he was placed on the trap, there was an audible "click" as his body weight activated a lever. The mechanism pulled a plug from a washtub filled with water and it began to pour from the upper tank into a lower one. When enough water had spilled out, the counterweights fell, pulling the hinged post from beneath the trapdoor.

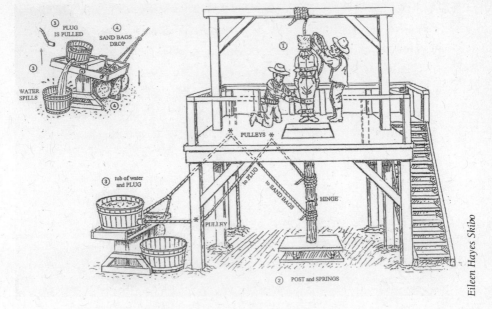

Eileen Hayes Skibo

RENDITION OF HORN'S GALLOWS

Horn stood erect with his hands clenched tightly, waiting for the trap to spring. It took thirty-five seconds before the post was pulled and the prisoner dropped through the trapdoor. Horn's neck was broken in the fall, but his heart continued to beat for sixteen minutes. He was allowed to hang for another four minutes before being cut down and handed over to the undertaker.

The following morning Horn's remains were claimed by his brother Charles and shipped to Boulder, Colorado, for interment. He was buried in the Columbia Cemetery, with Charles, his sweetheart Glendolene Kimmel, and his employer John Coble in attendance.

The most disturbing aspect of the Horn case was that he was quite possibly innocent of the killing of Willie Nickell. His confession, obtained by getting Horn into a drunken condition which the lawman knew would lead to baseless boasting, was unconscionable and the confession should not have been admitted in evidence. Even the most aggressive appeals campaign in the annals of the West, however, could not overturn the conviction. But even if Horn wasn't hanged for the murder of Nickell, he most likely would have met that fate for another one of his murders.

Bibliography

General References

Duff, Charles. *A Handbook on Hanging*. London: Putnam, 1961.

Horan, James D., and Paul Sann. *Pictorial History of the Wild West*. New York: Bonanza Books, 1954.

Koestler, Arthur. *Reflections on Hanging*. New York: MacMillan, 1957.

McLoughlin, Denis. *Wild and Woolly: An Encyclopedia of the Old West*. New York: Barnes & Noble Books, 1975.

Mencken, August. *By The Neck, A Book of Hangings*. New York: Hastings House, 1942.

Nash, Jay R. *Encyclopedia of Western Lawmen and Outlaws*. New York: Da Capo Press, 1989.

Teeters, Negley, and Jack Hedblom. *Hang by the Neck: The Legal Use of Scaffold and Noose, Gibbet, Stake*. Springfield, Ill.: Charles Thomas, 1967.

Thrapp, Dan L. *Encyclopedia of Frontier Biography, in Three Volumes*. Lincoln, Nebr.: University of Nebraska Press, 1988.

Frenchman Hanged for Murdering a "Lady"

Elliott, Russell R. *History of Nevada*. Lincoln, Nebr.: University of Nebraska Press, 1973.

Millian, John. *Life and Confession of John Millian: Convicted as the Murderer of Julia Bulette as Given by Him to his Attorney.* Virginia, Nev.: Lammon, Gregory & Palmer, 1868.

Virginia City (Nev.) *Territorial Enterprise:* January 22, 1867; April 19, 1867; April 24, 1867; April 25, 1867; May 25, 1867; May 31, 1867; June 1, 1867; June 4, 1867; June 6, 1867; June 27, 1867; July 6, 1867; February 8, 1868; April 28, 1868.

Moore and His Gang Lynched in Laramie

Carroll, Murray L. "Judge Lynch Rides the Rails; Bringing the Law to Laramie." *True West,* October 1995, 12.

Cheyenne (Wyo.) *Daily Evening Leader:* January 22, 1868; May 6, 1868; October 19–22, 1868.

Engebretson, Doug. *Empty Saddles, Forgotten Names: Outlaws of the Black Hills and Wyoming.* Aberdeen, S.Dak.: North Plains Press, 1984.

Gorzalka, Ann. *Wyoming's Territorial Sheriffs.* Glendo, Wyo.: High Plains Press, 1998.

Escaped Convicts Meet Their Fate

Bristow, Allen P. "Break Out!" *Old West,* Winter 1998, 26.

Carson City (Nev.) *Register,* September 18, 1871.

Elliott, Russell R. *History of Nevada.* Lincoln, Nebr.: University of Nebraska Press, 1973.

Gold Hill (Nev.) *Evening News:* September 30, 1871; October 1, 1871; October 4, 1871; October 6, 1871; October 10, 1871.

Hume, James B., and John N. Thacker. "Report of JAS. B. HUME and JNO. N. THACKER, Special Officers, Wells, Fargo & Co's Express,

Covering a Period of Fourteen Years, giving losses by Train
Robbers, Stage Robbers and Burglaries, and a full description and
record of all NOTED CRIMINALS Convicted of Offenses Against
Wells, Fargo & Company Since November 5th, 1970." San
Francisco, California: H. S. Crocker & Co., 1885.

"Buffalo Curly" Assassinates "Wild Bill"

Adams Museum and House. "Legendary Characters and Notable
People: Jack McCall." adamsmuseumandhouse.org/answers/
jackmccall.html.

Harrison, Fred. "The Trial of Jack McCall." *Real West,* November
1966, 20.

Hart, George. "Jack McCall: Frontier Enigma." *Real West,* November
1972, 18.

McClintock, John S. *Pioneer Days in the Black Hills.* Norman, Okla.:
University of Oklahoma Press, 1939.

Roosevelt Inn. "Trial of Jack McCall." www.rosyinn.com/5100a52
.htm.

Rosa, Joseph G. "Draw It Tighter, Marshal." *Old West,* Summer 1971, 6.

Turner, Thadd. "The Shooting of Wild Bill." *True West,*
August–September 2001, 42.

———. "Although his life was full of wild and woolly adventures,
Wild Bill Hickok is best known for one day in Deadwood." *Wild
West,* February 2003, 16.

Yankton (Dakota Territory) *Dakotian,* March 1–2, 1877.

Yankton Daily Press & Dakotan. "The Murky Tale Of A Legendary Old
West Killing—And Yankton's Overrated Role In This Episode Of

Frontier History." www.yankton.net/stories/091599/bus_wildbill
.html.

John D. Lee Pays for the Mountain Meadows Massacre

Altman, Larry. "Mountain Meadows Massacre." *Real West,* November
1958, 26.

Gillespie, L. Kay. *The Unforgiven.* Salt Lake City, Utah: Signature
Books, 1991.

McLane, Bruce. "What Happened at Mountain Meadows?" *True
Western Adventures,* October 1966, 20.

Salt Lake City Deseret News, March 28, 1877.

Salt Lake City Tribune, May 23, 1877.

Sasser, Charles W. "Massacre at Mountain Meadows." *Old West,* Fall
1989, 14.

The Pickled Parrott

Arlandson, Lee. "When 'Big Nose' George Parrott Was Hung." *Pioneer
West,* June 1972, 40.

Breihan, Carl W. "Big Nose George Parrott." *Real West,* September
1968, 26.

Engebretson, Doug. *Empty Saddles, Forgotten Names: Outlaws of the
Black Hills and Wyoming.* Aberdeen, S.Dak.: North Plains Press,
1984.

Gorzalka, Ann. *Wyoming's Territorial Sheriffs.* Glendo, Wyo.: High
Plains Press, 1998.

Holben, Richard. "Pickling Outlaws was a Form of Lynch Law
Vengeance." *Frontier West,* December 1974, 22.

Mason, John. "Hanging of Big Nose George." *Real West*, January 1960, 17.

McClintock, John S. *Pioneer Days in the Black Hills*. Norman, Okla.: University of Oklahoma Press, 1939.

Patterson, Richard. *The Train Robbery Era*. Boulder, Colo.: Pruett Publishing Company, 1991.

Spring, Agnes W. *The Cheyenne and Black Hills Stage and Express Routes*. Lincoln, Nebr.: University of Nebraska Press, 1948.

Wolfe, George D. "Curtains for Big Nose George." *True West*, April 1961, 18.

The Pond Brothers Lynched by Vigilantes

Bristow, Allen P. "Those Damn Postcards." *Old West*, Spring 1997, 40.

Cline, Don. "Billy Leroy: The Original Billy the Kid." *Frontier Times*, February 1985, 25.

Rasch, Philip J. "Billy Leroy—Incompetent Highwayman." *Real West*, March 1988, 6.

Reilly, Jim. "They Died on Lonesome Road." *Real West*, July 1962, 8.

Rocky Mountain (Colo.) *News:* January 15, 1881; May 25, 1881.

Saguache (Colo.) *Chronicle*: May 18, 1878; May 27, 1881; July 1, 1881; September 2, 1881.

Gilbert and Rosengrants Hanged by Double Twitch-Up Gallows

Denver Daily News, July 30, 1881.

One Lynched and Five Hanged for the Bisbee Massacre

Ball, Larry D. *Desert Lawmen: The High Sheriffs of New Mexico and Arizona, 1846–1912.* Albuquerque, N.Mex.: University of New Mexico Press, 1992.

Born, Dewey E. "The Bisbee Massacre cost five lives—actually 11 lives, after the six men responsible were punished." *Wild West,* June 2006, 60.

Carson, Xanthus. "The Bisbee Massacre." *Westerner,* November 1970, 48.

Kildare, Maurice. "The Bisbee Massacre Hanging." *Real West,* August 1871, 16.

Phoenix Herald: December 10, 1883; December 11, 1883; December 15, 1883; December 20, 1883; December 22, 1883.

Tucson (Ariz.) *Weekly Citizen,* March 29, 1884.

Poor Andy! From Slave to Grave

Rocky Mountain (Colo.) *News,* July 27, 1886.

First Woman Hanged in Nevada

Elko (Nev.) *Independent:* January 27, 1889; February 3, 1889; March 17, 1889; March 23, 1889; March 24, 1889; June 13, 1890; June 22, 1890; June 23, 1890; July 5, 1890.

Elliott, Russell R. *History of Nevada.* Lincoln, Nebr.: University of Nebraska Press, 1973.

Nevada State Library and Archives. "Ten Cases of the Nevada Supreme Court; Case 5: State v. Potts." dmla.clan.lib.nv.us/docs/nsla/archives/top10/case-05.htm.

Virginia City (Nev.) *Territorial Enterprise:* April 25, 1890; June 6, 1890.

White Pine (Nev.) *News,* June 29, 1890.

Enoch Davis Dies by Firing Squad

Gillespie, L. Kay. *The Unforgiven.* Salt Lake City, Utah: Signature
Books, 1991.

Salt Lake City Tribune, September 14, 1894; September 15, 1894.

Wife Murderer Charles H. Thiede Hanged

Gillespie, L. Kay. *The Unforgiven.* Salt Lake City, Utah: Signature
Books, 1991.

Salt Lake City Tribune: August 6 1896; August 8, 1896.

Parker Punished for the Jailbreak Murder

Ball, Larry D. *Desert Lawmen: The High Sheriffs of New Mexico and
Arizona, 1846–1912.* Albuquerque, N.Mex.: University of New
Mexico Press, 1992.

Edwards, Harold L. "A Rope for Cowboy Fleming Parker." *Wild West,*
October 2000, 52.

Martin, Lovell. "Statement of Love Marvin's [sic] Confession; Prescott,
Arizona, March 22, 1897." Sharlot Hall Museum, Archives and
Library. DB10, f.4, i.17.

Patterson, Richard. *The Train Robbery Era.* Boulder, Colo.: Pruett
Publishing Company, 1991.

Prescott (Ariz.) *Journal Miner:* February 9, 1897; February 17, 1897;
February 24, 1897; April 28, 1897; May 12, 1897; May 19, 1897;
May 26, 1897; June 2, 1897; June 11, 1897; June 23, 1897; June 28,
1897; June 30, 1897; June 8, 1898.

Rasch, Philip J. "Fleming Jim Parker, Arizona Desperado." *NOLA Quarterly* VII, no. 1 (Summer 1982), 1.

Secrest, William B. "Tell the Boys I Died Game." *True West,* February 1980, 28.

Stano, Mary G. "The Lawless Trial of Fleming Parker." *True West,* December 1990, 42.

Yuma (Ariz.) *Sentinel,* May 15, 1897.

A Hanging Done Right

Boise (Idaho) *Daily Statesman:* June 24 1898; June 25, 1898; August 30, 1925.

Idaho World, June 24, 1898.

Beheaded by the Noose

Burton, Jeffrey. "Tom Ketchum and His Gang." *Wild West,* December 2001, 32.

Cortesi, Lawrence. "The Black Jack Ketchum Gang." *Pioneer West,* November 1978, 6.

Elman, Robert. *Badmen of the West.* Secaucus, N.J.: Castle Books, 1974.

Galbraith, West. *Death on the Gallows.* Silver City, N.Mex.: High-Lonesome Books, 2002.

Reiss, Malcolm. "Blackjack Ketchum: The End of His Gang." *True Western Adventures,* June 1961, 20.

Youngs, C. Daniel. "How Black Jack Lost His Head." *Real West,* November 1958, 46.

The Last Hanging in Prescott, Arizona

Arizona Republican, August 1, 1903.

Ball, Larry D. *Desert Lawmen: The High Sheriffs of New Mexico and Arizona, 1846–1912*. Albuquerque, N.Mex.: University of New Mexico Press, 1992.

Born, Dewey. "On July 31, 1903, Sheriff Joe Roberts did his duty—he pulled the lever at the last execution in Prescott." *Wild West*, February 2001, 12.

Coburn, Walt. "Dual Hanging in Arizona." *Badman*, Annual 1971, 40.

The Hanging of an Innocent Man?

Brown, Larry K. *You Are Respectfully Invited to Attend My Execution*. Glendo, Wyo.: High Plains Press, 1997.

Browning, Dwain. "Tom Horn." *Great West*, October 1968, 18.

Carlson, Chip. "Tom Horn on Trial." *Wild West*, October 2001, 32.

Carson, John. "Tom Horn—Was a Hero or Villain Hanged?" *True West*, November–December 1960, 26.

Engebretson, Doug. *Empty Saddles, Forgotten Names: Outlaws of the Black Hills and Wyoming*. Aberdeen, S.Dak.: North Plains Press, 1984.

Koller, Joe. "Tom Horn: Man of Mystery." *Real West*, March 1971, 38.

McClintock, John S. *Pioneer Days in the Black Hills*. Norman, Okla.: University of Oklahoma Press, 1939.

Repp, Ed E. "The Mystery of Tom Horn." *The West*, November 1968, 30.

Index

About the Author

R. Michael Wilson has been researching the Old West for fifteen years, following a quarter century as a law enforcement officer in Southern California. He holds an Associate Degree in Police Science, a Bachelor's Degree in Criminology, a Master's Degree in Public Administration, and a Juris Doctorate degree.

Wilson is an active member of the National Outlaw Lawman Association (NOLA) and Western Writers of America (WWA). He has seven history books to his credit, all in his area of interest and expertise—crime and punishment in America's early West. His works represent his philosophy to report "the truth, the whole truth, and nothing but the truth."